KEEP BLACK HISTORY ALIVE 12 TRIBES

★★★★★★★★★★★★★★★

LET US MAKE MAN

NOW GOD'S LAW
1,000 YEARS PEACE
AT LAST TRUTH

Fortney Encyclical History Ed. Co.

Copyright © 2025 by Albert Fortney Jr., Let Us Make Man

All rights reserved.

No part of this book may be reproduced or used in any manner whatsoever without the prior written permission of the copyright owner, except for the use of brief quotations in a review.

Printed in the United States of America

ISBN: 979-8-218-70585-5

TABLE OF CONTENTS

1   Introduction   i

2   The Why of Let Us Make Man   1

3   The Awareness of Let Us Make Man   17

4   Yacub's Scientific Creation of a Man   38

    Malcolm X's Hajj [pilgrimage] to Mecca with an

    Important message: America on a suicide path

5   Identity Identifying Lesson of Lessons   84

6   Nubian Americans Identity Rise DNA Proof   109

INTRODUCTION

We, the *Fortney Encyclical History Ed. Co.,* have nothing but love for all of humanities no racist fantastic accomplishments, and beneficial achievements of mankind. It is important to note that many African American **titled** black men learn the value of his hidden cultural-history like it came to the "Black Prince of his people," Islamic teacher Malcolm X, while in prison. How intelligent was Malcolm X? He was a genius with an **IQ of 165,** which places him in a class for gifted students (also known as "Krelboynes"). Did Malcolm X go to Harvard? Yes, in the finale of "Malcolm in the Middle" titled "Graduation," Malcolm X was accepted into Harvard and attends the University. He even secures a job as a janitor at Harvard to help cover his tuition.

Similar, was only by going to prison in 1964 at 22 years old. Was for punching in the face a white gas station owner and done 16 months in prison; having plenty of time to think, Negro Albert Fortney Jr. age 22, didn't graduate with his college-prep in High School near graduation being suspended, for a stupid fight with a young white gym teacher. However, researched in prison on "black-awareness history." My prison classification was above average, I.Q. 125+, and told could be a C.E.O in insurance. At 19 years old in Denver, Colorado took Civil Service test got a 98% right. But learned of a **"Nubian identity"** 61 yrs. ago. At present, I'm 83 years old until July 26th, who writes for the betterment and **equal rights** for everyone. Has now written 12 vital history books plus a fiction total 13 books, **"Historian Author Credentials."**

We should make sure the system works for all of us. The republican "mentally unstable 78 years old **dictator Trump** want to be," has no concept of a plan that's definitely good for the people;

especially in black impoverished communities at the bottom of America's political totem-pole. If you're not a Native American, you're born from immigrants as this county is composed of all immigrants except for the white man's black Nubian ex-slaves. And now today, we must put women back in control of their bodies with health-care. Trump racism, is really a direct, majority, **black-public** health, matter of **death-problem.** Including himself Trump's first term cabinet as president were all **Ashkenazi** Jews, were they not? But now they all deny being, asks the obvious question why? Having a <u>Satan</u> reputation, lust for money and leech of power.

    We **grow,** by values of good principals and deeds. Because if not, America won't stop black's **despair** without representatives with values of character, and not characters with **lies contrary** to the **truth** for the people is not the aim of the **constitution** to govern America for her right to betterment. And for generations to come, to even those who don't agree with you; but a mutual **"respect"** of all without any racist <u>white supremacy hoax</u>; trying to extend **indefinitely,** his end prophecy. So why **"deprive"** those who built you America; is it not against the laws of nature and God with their blood, sweat and tears, and to do so with loathsome **corruption,** detestable **crimes,** and **evil blood-games** towards **extinction** of the black man in **hell,** "Your **Time** is Up!!!"

    You be the judge, to what was the worst wrong of evil atrocities each race has done to another? But the one that stands out the worst suffered was done to the yellow man, by the white man we've all agreed here; was dropping of mass death, that could have been avoided, done another way, with a threat done on a deserted island, was **atomic bombs** twice on the yellow Asian race; regardless in war with the so-called reason to save white lives and end the war earlier; wasn't dropped on white man Germany, to save lives ending WWII earlier... why?

    Today's Israel Jew Netanyahu, prime minister of the Israelis is no more than a **criminal** also a **dictator** trying to dodge prison.

Whose military aim is to destroy all of Gaza and claim as Israeli; America must discontinue to support with finance and war-materials that's decimating Palestinian's with illegal continued occupied settlements; with the excuse of war to root-out Hamas. Whose results only amount to the inhumane despair of Palestinian innocent citizens, against Netanyahu's genocidal-apartheid practices of Gaza's now 85% devastated a wasteland; with unrecovered dead bodies of men, women, children and babies trapped under ruins of debris; disease; and famine is his criminal evil; much-less the unnecessary bombing of all most all hospitals and schools. Gaza has no military force, nothing able to fight back, hoping a future state to protect her civilians.

Netanyahu must be eliminated, removed from office to end the war to save Gaza and Israel as separate States. On TV President Biden hugged Netanyahu, upon meeting is very questionable.

The devil even to himself whites say, "poor devil," who murder to claim black lands as his, whitewashing black achievements along with black history, and the Jew lying and fabricating of converting is really of stealing the African black Hebrew Jew religion as Israeli Jews; can only be of Satan; the scripture define as "the father of lies and a murderer." Is all about the white man Islam prophesized to rule for 6,000 years would begin after the black man's rule of the planet; would end about this time for a 1,000 years world-wide peace perhaps saved by the Nubian American's inside political endeavors of America's democracy; is our sincere committed belief.

It's not about what you want to hear, it's what you need to **"know."** Just like it seems to relate to why whites despise all other races with color, behind their lack of color and by blacks saying **"let us make man"** in the scriptures of the Holy Bible, the black man created in physical written words said; not our loving God to angels who needed no help, or with the white man's obvious hoax of evolution of coming from an **"ape."** Why would white people hate coming from blacks when all races stem from Africa unless there is another reason; that was in-bred or a hereditary trait handed down from a story told by the "Nation of Islam of Yacub" and his devoted constituents taking 600 years to do, is not out of contents of factual truth but the white man and Euro-Israeli Jews calls just a myth.

Incubated before birth an embryo, we had no knowledge **how** we was created. Now we are here and all of us on this earth were created, making no difference in skin color at that time so it shouldn't **now** only respect for our creator under God. This is not racist talk "let us make man" creation by black-man was **God's plan;** to allow us freedom to come to **Him,** living His laws! White-man's deadly **super-ego** needs to be put aside! Because "Black lives matter" and no more ancient-biblical **prophesized,** too many "I can't breathe" today!

It could be that the prophesized "trouble-maker of the world white man," with a despicable **whitewashing** of history; lies with Christianity's black characters all depicted as white, is his unreasonable **vengeance** that's supposedly not a myth; concerns the biblical truth from Cush's Ancient statement, let us make man enlightenment for "Nubian Americans and world-wide acknowledgement;" that Almighty God has allowed to manifest proving He is God to change.

This book was compiled with relentless researched facts from myths for the purpose of proof/evidence that perhaps can't be disputed, nor ignored by white man scholars, or his historian's wickedness. Not in retaliation but to remind, where you come from. And so begins, "Let Us Make Man." Almost, every time the subject matter of the "ex-slave," a down-spirit of black man's suffering, only "blood-games" seems felt by whites in their cruelty, but an ultimate in black's humiliation of enslavement is **tumultuous** (tending to incite violent agitation of mind or feelings), won't forget. If only for a split-second it's felt; like a reminder and not an apology especially and regardless of black **prominence,** by known white-supremacists; inferring, supposedly that our black man's place, is at the bottom of

America's bias and <u>racist</u> societies, totem-pole!

Not to mention, the tumultuous feeling we black people suppress; also showing the black man Jesus Christ a Nubian, as a white man Jesus around the world, and besides seeing the three great pyramids of Gaza, Egypt (black man's Kemet), in Africa that's black man's "pride and Joy" known the "world-over," portrayed behind a whiteman <u>imposter</u> shown as the builder! That, "Old tumultuous feeling" raises from deep within, that may forgive within the black man's heart with suppression, but the mind will never forget these <u>humiliating</u> **atrocities** from the U.S. **"KKK"** (Klu-Klux-Klan) **Horror** to us, WHO BUILT THIS NATION!!! GOD KNOWS…

And shown here, also in this nation is **"Proof/evidence" – for law in any court** is what matters to defend, not speculation… "History, the black man prophecies, fact, faith leaders & proof/evidence," totally shows that at their worst; the white man is the world's <u>trouble</u>-maker is in his **"nature,"** and on earth only 6,000 years whose **ruling** time is up; much less Euro-pale face **Jews** (from southwestern Asia & [southeastern Europe]), because they **won't** obey, **black man's original,** first written **Holy Bible** of "God & nations ruling man-gods." God's law sure, is emphatically against; **abhorrent** <u>homosexuality</u> & <u>same</u>-<u>sex</u> marriage <u>foolishness</u>, period, amen.

Just as, no one can refute: Outside the situation looking in, the black and brown ideology of WWII's racial <u>hate</u> basics was, a "white man's Caucasian <u>war</u>" erupted against; Asiatic-Euro pale-face Jews in Germany. Jews were **"<u>anti</u>-<u>creating</u>"** of the white man by blacks, just as Semite Jews are **"<u>anti</u>-<u>black</u> man"**… but in original God's law, these <u>racial wars,</u> **"will"** all **End!** Trust a 34 convictions Trump, literally smacking to death, innocent black folk around but in real life to actually face death; God knows, is about to be punched right back with his constituencies, by "stout and fearless blacks" answering back, much less God's catastrophes… HALLELUJAH!

Also interestingly fantastic you must read before leaving you here, written by us is "A Company of History" like: *"Nubians Originators of World History"*. Available on Amazon.

****

CHAPTER 1
The Why of Let us Make Man

The Godly seed that burst into roots forming the racial tree of all humanity, was Africa. We cannot gloss over the fact nor give a false acceptance, whether you believe in "Let Us Make Man" or not; all races stem from the **"Mother of Mankind** Africa.**"** Africa's Sahara Sudan

"Biblical Cush (or Kush)" is the cradle of all civilizations that was often called Ethiopia. From the bottom-up man will save humanity from mass destruction the white man with greed and the lie is taking us to, like it's his way or no-way he's chosen deception without his love of truth for **God's Laws!!!**

Why do Americans use the term Caucasian to describe white people? They say, it's a holdover from earlier times and not really a preferred term anymore. The US census for example does not provide Caucasian as a choice. But as far as they know the broadening of the meaning to "white people" happened in anthropological/sociological circles in 18/19th century Europe. Or could it have been that too much attention wasn't wanted, or noticeable to believe at that time directed to black awareness movements or Biblical "let us make man," especially from the Islamic point of view Nation of Islam's **Yakub:** definition of **creation** of the **Caucasian!**

White folk say, somewhere around modern day **Armenia,** groups descended from Noah's children were thought of as **Caucasian,** though it would be white people specifically that ended up as the dominant associated with the term. This was given credence by old medieval stereotypes and folklore about the area among Europeans idea that it was the origin of the white race.

Remember, that the same Caucasian so-called devils who enslaved our forefathers and ourselves, diluted the **truth** in the **Bible** like the Noah excuse for slavery of the black man. When they translated it out of the Greek tongues into the English language. It was originally given to Hebrews by Ethiopians (Moslems). Also remember, no longer Negroes nor African Americans but correct identity as **Nubian** Americans were put in slavery, separated from his motherland, his culture, his God and his language. At the same time Caucasian devil's partner in crime Satan white-Jews hid **"guilt"** pointing fingers and **lies** accusing others, being anti-Semite and crooked. A white superior only in wickedness, a trouble maker, and giving death!

America has become overrun with immorality and corruption. God punishes with mother-nature catastrophes if nothing else a warning... The white man in general is pathetic and pitiful with hate. Having to depend and rely on in history with fear, hate, imitating, lying, stealing, murder and war to get ahead but claims being "white superior" the hoax over all other races; is the absolute truth that only a real **Devil** would do! Like profound **racist** chump, Donald Trump.

Shem was considered to be the father of all Asian peoples, and from his name in Latin (Sem), we get the term Semites. However it was later decided that Semitic peoples as an ethnolinguistic group had a Caucasian origin is not correct, however having a **black** origin.

"Let us make man," said Yakub. Ya'qub (Yakub) is the Arabic variant of the name of the Biblical Patriarch known as Jacob in the English language versions of the Bible, and Ya'qob in Biblical Hebrew. Fard Muhammad's Yacub has some parallels to the Biblical Jacob's role as the father of the **"12 Tribes of Israel:"**

The 12 tribes of Israel were prophesized to split apart in 1 Kings 11:31-39. The split actually happened in 1 Kings 12:16-24. The **"Northern Kingdom of Israel"** of the twelve are as follow:

1. **Reuben** – Seminole Indians/Aboriginal Australians
2. **Simeon** – Dominicans
3. **Zebulon** – Guatemalans/Panamanians
4. **Issachar** – Mexicans
5. **Gad** – North American Indians
6. **Asher** – Columbians/Brazilians/Argentines/Venezuelans
7. **Napthali** – Hawaiians/Samoans/Tongans/Fijians
8. **Ephraim** – Puerto Ricans
9. **Manasseth** – Cubans

"**Southern Kingdom of Judah**" continues as follows:

10. **Judah** – Negroes/Colored/African Americans proper identity:

Nubian Americans

11. **Benjamin** – Jamaicans/West Indians/Trinidadians
12. **Levi** – Haitians

The "**14th Book**" of the "**APOCRYPHA**" was removed from the King James Version Bible in 1885; leaving the now 66 books. It told of the removed **2 Esdras 13: 40-45,** how the **Northern** tribes sailed to **Arsareth** a.k.a. **America** (North, South, and Central Americas). **The Kingdom of Israel**" was first the star Samaria, then Shechem, Jerash, Jaffa, Belt El, and Jericho etc. However, the **Southern** tribes remained in the East; for a period of time, which was "**The Kingdom of Judah**" (Black Mans), the star city of **Jerusalem,** then Lachish, Hebron, and Beersheba etc. "**The Philistine States**" Gaza (West Bank), Ashkenlon, Ashod etc.

The early history of Jerusalem is rooted in the Holy Bible. Pilgrimage to the Islamic city "**Mecca,**" that Judaism made a holy city over "**3,000 years ago.**" It has Muslim, the Christian Bible and Euro-Jewish associations. But Palestinians call on Muslims States to "**protect**" the "Holy City" that belongs to all Muslims.

It is the law to kill anyone who denies Torah. The Christians belong to the denying ones of the Torah, **Talmud.** Ashkenazi Euro-Jewish Zionist flooded **Palestine** with crimes against humanity, coming from Europe with **violence** to conquer and supposedly cleanse [remove] the indigenous people of Palestine.

According to **Exodus 11:7**, Negros, Judeans African Americans and Nubian Egyptians, Africans, and Nubian Americans, are not the same people coming from different places like Egypt and Israel although they look "most similar" (in today's DNA proof/evidence). **1 Maccabees 12:20-21** (KJV), "Areus King of the Lacedemonians to Onis" the high priest, greeting: 21 It is found in writing that the Lacedemonians and Jews are brethren, and that they are of stock of **Abraham.**

1 Maccabees 12: 20-21 (good news Bible with Apocrypha) "King Arius of **Sparta** to Onis the high priest greetings. 21 We have found a document about the **Spartans** and the [the bold emphasis is this book's author] The Spartans were Black. The movie **"300"** should have had an all-black caste, but of course, white imitators' objection was not in that direction, having to deny a true project in history for white entertainment is just like Shakespeare, Hannibal, Napoleon, Alexander the Great, Mozart and Beethoven much less Cleopatra or Christ etc., who all for certain were Blacks!

This is not said nor written in **"hate nor racism,"** toward the white or Semite race just to feel better but its truth might save someone's **life** in despair. And to bring to the surface true history lessons, for its curriculum studies in classroom education. Emphasize no more serious white man superior hoax **demeaning** and **killing** black people, under pretense of saving savages; the Nubian Americans of African descent, from their **ignorance and lack of intelligence,** "little white lie;" while white men superiors look the other way, as in disbelief a mockery!

It is known today with modern science traced back and discovered, that modern black man lived 200,000 to far back as 300,000 years ago on the continent of Africa. Through time as he created civilizations their rulers of nations were often called gods. It was a "man-god" and **not Almighty God** who said, "Let us make man;" because God doesn't need help to do anything; who created the whole universe by himself!!! And so, was it really **"Yakub"** words referred to and said, **"let us make man?"** And so, who was Yakub if in the Bible? In ancient times black man ruled the world there were no white men, only light-brown and yellow, white as you got.

There is no time now for foolishness history, as the world is heading, almost at the brink of destruction. Wise men tell no tales. Heed the facts of warning, not speculation for the new day.

Yakub, also known as Jacob in the Biblical narrative, was the son of Is'haq (Isaac) and the grandson of Ibrahim (Abraham). He is mentioned in the Quran (Surah 12) and his story is told through the narrative of his son Yusuf (Joseph). Who was Jesus to Jacob? Matthew began Jesus' lineage with Abraham and named each father in 41 generations ending in Matthew 1:16: "And Jacob begat **Joseph the husband of Mary,** of whom was born Jesus, who is called "Christ." Joseph descended from David through his son Solomon.

Here is the blood line Jesus came from. Matthew begins by calling Jesus the **son of David,** indicating that he was an Israelite; both stock phrases, in which son means descendant, calling to mind the promises God made to David and to Abraham. Here's how Jesus fits into Islam. Muslims regard Jesus (peace be upon him) as one of the great prophets who brought divine guidance to humanity before the prophet Muhammad (peace be upon him and his family).

The Jews are called Israelites because the Israelites were named after their ancestor, Jacob/Israel, who was the grandson of Abraham. They were organized into 12 tribes of Israel. And Jesus was descendant from the black tribe of **"Judah."** The prophecy was significant to the original (black) Hebrew Jewish faith as they believed this meant the black **"Messiah"** will come from the **tribe of Judah (Nubian Americans).** And surfacing knowledge of the White-Man's "hidden truth," so as to depict as himself in History to deceive; "divide & conquer" and rule was prophesized by "African-

Asiatic Holy-Men" of Christianity and Islamic "Nation of Islam."

Just because we don't understand them, there are things in life's journey that surface upon the waters of "knowledge and wisdom" you may not be able to understand. Doesn't make them wrong or obscure to truth; even though explained many times, blocked by the way perhaps you was taught or indoctrinated or left-out you just reject, that's a mystery of man or history. But, if you was raised with basic "good values" produces good character to accept the unknown with Shemites (or Semites), the original Israelites were of the **Black** race and the biblical Abraham (or Abram) was a black Shemite (a descendant of Shem) and not Euro-White Jews.

Abraham was the father of both the Hebrew/Israelite and the **Arab** Nation. According to the biblical account Moses' parents were from **the tribe of Levi,** one of the groups of Egypt called Hebrews. God (perhaps history may show was the **"man-god"** of his nation white man changed in the KJV of the Holy Bible to deceive) chose the Israelites as His **"Chosen People"** and freed from slavery because God love them and because God made promises to their ancestors, the biblical patriarchs (founder of a **tribe** [let us make man]): Abraham, Isaac, and **Jacob.**

There are other books written about Yakub: *The Father Of The White Race:* A research in World History. This book examines whether Caucasians are genetically inclined to hate and practice racism against people of color. Book of Yakub: *Father of the Caucasian People:* Some say this book is a great read for open-mined people who love to explore the unknown and question humanity and religion. [Sounds kind of doubtful and negative perhaps but praises the artful way written].

It was originally given to Hebrews by Ethiopians (Moslems), Genesis 1:26 Let us make man. Genesis 10:1-32 generations of the sons of Noah after the flood [Approx. 12,000 years ago]. Matthew 1:1-25 – The genealogy of Jesus Christ – Abraham Numbers 12:1-16 – Moses married a Cushite [Nubian] woman… Revelation – 19:1-21, [Is

America 19:2 **"The Black Race in Africa,"** is in Acts 17:26 – And hath made from one blood all nations of men for to dwell on all the face of the earth, and hath determined the time before appointed, and the bounds and the bounds of their habitation; ... Who was the son of man in the Bible Luke 9:26 – Jesus Christ.

According to **National Geographic** the genetic make-up of modern Europeans, which includes what is often referred to as "Caucasian" features, was primarily establish around **6,000** years ago by a wave of Neolithic farmers migrating from the area of present Turkey [may not be accurate for sure speculation and not the recorded island of Patmos, Greeks in the Aegean Sea] who mixed with earlier hunter gatherer populations already living in Europe. This essentially marked the **"First appearance of the Caucasian"** genetic profile as we understand it today.

DNA recovered from ancient skeletons reveals, genetic makeup of modern Europe, established around **4,500 BC,** in the mid-Neolithic **6,500 years ago.** The evidence also emphatically makes it clear that the first Europeans were **dark skinned (black man).** Olalde et al. (2014) provides conclusive genetic evidence that hunter gatherers in Mesolithic (between the earliest and mid) Europe were dark skinned highly pigmented some with light (blue) eyes. I am a dark skinned man the author, interjecting he and his baby sister has brown eyes with a light blue rim around them strange hah! ...

Homo erectus and the Smithsonian Institution's Human Origins Program, of Black Europeans of African ancestry, or Afro-European **Moors,** refers to people in Europe who trace their ancestry as **"Sub-Saharan Nubia, Africa."** The term Caucasian is not an ethnicity (a people classified according to common traits and customs), is **a racial category** that was introduced in the **1780s** by members of the Gottingen school of history – notably Christoph Meiners in 1785 and Johann Friedrich Blumenbach in 1795 – it had originally referred in a narrow sense to the native inhabitants of the Caucasus region.

Patmos is located in the Aegean Sea is the northern most island in the Dodecanese Islands. It's also known as the island of the Apocalypse and Jerusalem of the Aegean. A part of the country of Greece and about 38 miles from the mainland of Turkey, so its left up to you, be the judge whether Patmos or Turkey; is where Islamic Nation of Islam say scientist Yakub created the Aryan race. Allah means God!

Who is the son of man in the Bible – Luke 9:26 is Jesus. The Black Race – (Acts 17:26) - And He made, one man into every nation of mankind to live on all the face of the earth, having determined allotted periods, and the boundaries of their dwelling place.

Only the truth is said next and not hate or racism, it is the false-Jews who promote the filth of Hollywood. The false-Jews bring you down in moral strength promoting lesbianism homosexual draw the line, same sex marriage, and you call homophobic when you present the laws of God.

The Gottingen school of history, notably Christoph Meiners in 1785, and Johann Friedrich Blumenbach in 1795, had originally referred in a narrow sense to the native inhabitants of the Caucasus region. The Scottish genetically is closest to many of the genetic patterns found were similar to the genes found in **Gaels, Picts, Britons, and the Norse,** echoes the DNA of past kingdoms.

The modern French are descendants of mixtures including Romans, Celts, Iberians, Ligurians and Greeks in southern France, Germanic peoples arriving at the end of the Roman Empire such as the Franks and the Burgundians, and some Vikings who mixed with the Normans and settled mostly in Normandy in the 9th century. Brings up the question, are the Irish and Germans related? The Irish are **not Germanic, Slavic, or Latin.** They are Celtic. Linguistically, the Irish are one of the 6 Celtic ethnic groups: Irish, Scottish, Manx, Welsh, Cornish, and Breton.

So now, where are Native Americans originally from? **Northeast Asia –** who migrated over the Bering Strait land bridge no longer is capable not there, into North America probably during the last glacial period (about 30,000 – to 12,000 years ago). However, by 10,000 BC, they were preset in much of North, Central, and South America.

Are Russians considered Caucasian? Slavic groups account for more than 1/3of the total population of the Caucasus; they live in the north and consist mainly of Russians and Ukrainians. Then, there are such Indo-European groups as Kurds, Talysh, Tats, Greeks and Roma (Gypsies) distributed in various areas of the Caucasus.

The next question shouldn't have to be asked but we will. Where did Black humans come from? Homo-Sapiens most likely developed in the Horn of Africa, who said so white historian scholars; when black Africans **should know** say it was Sahara's Sudan Nubia/Ethiopia the biblical **"Cush,"** between 300,000 and 200,000 years ago. The oldest known evidence for anatomically modern humans (as of 2017) are **fossils found at Jebel Irhound, Morocco** (North Africa not the southern Horn of Africa) **dated about 360,000, years old.** Anatomically modern human remains of 8 individuals dated 300,000 years old, making them the oldest known remains categorized as "modern" (as of 2018).

Black-Jew's Hebrew religion is rooted in **the ancient near eastern region of also was black Canaan** (which today constitutes Israel [at that time considered Africa without the Suez Canal] and the **Palestinian** territories [today's Israeli's want to take-over by violence with the military]). **Judaism** emerged from the beliefs and practices of the people were known as **"Israel"** (Blacks).

What is considered now white classical, or White-Jew rabbinical (Rev. 2:9-10 **Satan's**), **Judaism** did not emerge until the 1st century AD. Revelation 2:9-10, I know thy works, and tribulation, and poverty, (but thou art rich) and I *know* the blasphemy of them which say they are Jews, and are not, but *are* the Synagogue of Satan. 10. – Fear none of those things which thou shalt suffer: behold, the devil shall cast *some* of you into prison…

Hence, why isn't Israel still not considered part of Africa to be exact when she sits on African's **"Tectonic Plate,"** with all past and present protest against just because white man say so; by a so-called they built, Suez Canal supposed separation of water when the large land mass **Madagascar** is separated off the east coast of Africa by 400 miles of water separation but still considered apart of Africa?

Then again, the so-called **"Middle-East"** is Euro-American **"geopolitical concept"** rather than a **"geographical"** formation. The older terms of "Near East" and "Far East are also **geopolitical** terms. **Israel** is a [wanna be] **nation** located along the border of the African/**Nubian** and Arabian **"Tectonic Plates."** So from a **"GEOLOGICAL"** standpoint, Israel is [also] part Sin Sub-plate and Arabian plate. So now from a *"technical geology,"* black man standpoint, Egypt is clearly part of the African **Continent** and **Nubian** plate and Israel is part of a border region on a smaller plate connected to the Nubian plate; places Israel part of Africa! But, however from a *"geopolitical* **bias** and **racist"** white man standpoint, Israel now part of the so-called "Middle-East Term." The white man's man-made **Suez Canal** water-way borders between Africa and the Middle East claims; is what separates Israel from the continent of Africa!

The white man's argument viewpoint is the Sinai Desert possession that belongs to Egypt, is mixing geography modern-day Israel and his non-scientific **"B.S. Politics."** Because our Nubian argument is that, **Madagascar** is separated by 400 hundred miles of Indian Ocean water from the coast of east Africa, and is still considered a major part of the African Continent!!! So what is this obvious visual conflicting display of water supposedly separating Israel 300 miles walking in the past before the canal; from Egypt to Israel considered part of Africa that a **Nubian Jesus Christ** may have walked once before mustn't be forgotten in **"History!!!"**

Most people today agree that Israel and Lebanon reside in West Asia but also agree they are technically on the African plate and should be considered **"Northern African countries."** And that being said, while the Jews and Israeli are undoubtedly an **Afro-Asiatic** people, Israel does struggle with somewhat of an identity crisis; please understand that the Israeli racist ruling class against innocent **Palestinian** citizens from Ben Gurion to Bennet, wanted for Israel what Mustafa Kamal wanted for Turkey (Minus Kemal's charisma and industry) they want to **Europeanize** (make white mans) Israel; just as corrupt dodging court **Netanyahu** (Prime Minister) wants to turn it and Gaza into their secular European country.

There is no such thing as an "African Sub Continent," sub under what way only what historian white scholars want it to stay is no more; now with the Fortney Encyclical History Ed. Co. on the set with its Nubian American platform are the originators of world history. We had a civilization with culture, dignity and with respect trading with **"gold"** over **"6,000 years ago,"** and traded with **"China"** at that, check it out you dig!!! And too many uninformed people have confused the Middle East mistakenly for a continent. Many others have confused it with Northern East Africa. Although the majority of the Middle East is situated in West Asia it still does not constitute the entirety of the region covering of **Africa** that contains **Israel** in the Levant. There's an important reason for this misconception; to believe was intervention of white control is **geopolitical racism.**

The origin of the Middle East concept is a **British** term that originated in the 1850s in a British India office. But the term became more widely used when an American naval strategist Alfred Thayer Mahan used the term in 1902 to designate the area between Arabia and India. So in the 20th century terminology took pace during World War II when Egypt was the site of allies supply center with a racist objective mind-set to demonize black people as modern day native savages. This a deep-rooted meaning, a geographical division that precedes the Eurocentric terminologies of the African Israel region, now Asian Middle East; the late North Africa which brings a lot of **confusion** and racial **hate** today. The dividing-line today between Africa and Asia incorrectly is the Suez **"rift"** (separation).

The disgusting, humiliating real reason white man's tactic

influenced Egyptian leaders they say Egypt is in the Middle East instead of Africa is because Egyptians are trying to disassociate themselves, that doesn't include the people from Africa; or black skin people of Sudan Africa as seen. If you look at any world map, Egypt is definitely in Northeast Africa. But first you have to realize the original name for Egypt is **"Kemet"** which initially means **"Land of the Blacks."**

The original inhabitants of Kemet were black Africans that came from the south following the flow of the Nile River which flows south to north from central Africa to the Mediterranean Sea [reason why is equatorial near the equator]. Egypt is the name given to Kemet by the **Greeks.** The Greeks conquered Kemet and then the Romans took it from the Greeks and the Arabs took it from the Romans. And so, those peoples that are controlling the country called behalf are conquerors who don't want to be known as black because Africans are looked at and as being unintelligent savages, which is a grave injustice to the African Continent and its black people falsely accused.

Now understand, Israel's actual location is in Africa and genetic Jews are African and Israel is the promise land. **Egyptian people** will tell you they consider themselves Africans and don't accept anything other, what out-siders say, commenting on their behalf to the contrary. The inhabitants of Egypt also say, they identify as Egyptians native to a land as proud Africans and to let you know Egypt is in the middle between Africa and Asia so they are very close to Arabia and the Levant in history and culture for thousands upon thousands of years as well as to other beautiful African places. Egyptians say only the **statesmen** and **diplomats** of the world, have their bias comments of Egypt.

Many settled in Egypt, after invaders destruction of the Black ancient Egyptian civilization. Hence, many of the very light skin Egyptians of today are **not native** Africans. Regardless, should still consider the term African their **title** and Egyptian their black **"identity."** Today's Egyptian doesn't forget that almost an equal number of Black African **slaves** died during the **Arab** slave trade compared to the Trans-Atlantic Caucasian and Euro-Jew slave trade that over **100,000,000 million "Black slaves died;"** to which many of them committed suicide chained to each other, rather continuing the racist, horrible inhumane abusive journey.

Just as Black Africans haven't forgotten their millions who perished in North Africa and the Middle East that if they show up in today's Egypt, Egyptians would most likely consider and call a **"breed"** (Arabic word for slave) like Europeans would; as Egypt had a **historically antagonistic** relationship with Black Africa in the past. Beside and ill-regards the great things Nubians did for Egypt. Seems perhaps ungrateful, when Nubians, was Egypt's great pharaohs in the 25th Dynasty of Egypt's greatest achievements.

And just as Israel is part of the Levant, Israel indeed was a vital part of Africa. We repeat or to be exact, Israel sits on part of the African **"Tectonic Plate."** Seems like the geographic issue is like the "white man vs. a nation Israeli state issue," is as **antagonistic** to Caucasians as, let us make man is by Nubian (Cushite) Africans.

There was a second kingdom of **"Judah"** formed from, some of the ancient Israelites in West Africa. Displayed on the 1747 map of Africa. But was changed why? The answer, it was changed to **hide** the actual descendants of the **Black Hebrew Israelites,** who escaped the Roman slavery and persecution in 70 AD. They did not run toward the Roman armies to the north, as we were taught in history classes which was a pathetic theory, taught by Europeans. This is no mind-game, all we want is the truth to be heard.

The question asked to white scholars writers of history was, "Is it possible a black man called a **man-god** ruling his nation said let us make man and created the **Caucasian white man** through a period of time with selected graftation and their answers were:

Ouachita Baptist University – In Genesis 1:26 God says, "Let us make man (Adam) in our image…" Many scholars and archeologists now agree Jesus was most likely a **brown-skinned, wooly-haired,**

brown-eyed man more akin to a "Middle Eastern Jewish" or an Arab man of 2024. However, a likely candidate for the first person that the Bible seems clearly to indicate that he clearly was **black-skinned** is the nation of **CUSH.**

Jesus was the son of Ham, the son of Noah. His descendants, the Cushites, are the inhabitants of "Africa south of Egypt." Often this is equated with Ethiopia but Nubia (North-Sudan) probably is more correct CNN 2021. **"There are no white people in the Bible."** Except, those stricken with leprosy. So why all characters in the Bible with white man depictions, are **lied-white???** What is the Caucasian white man trying to get across could it be hate retaliated being created by blacks; he resents with a vengeance to cover-up against all black and brown peoples not being and never can be a 13th tribe of Israel, he tries to enforce. **Honor thy mother and father or your days will be short upon this earth.** Nubians are people many of them having very light-skinned with always nappy-hair but most are dark-skinned. Ethiopians (People with burnt faces) actually come in multiple shades. Howard University School of Divinity.

Nubian American's ancestry history from Sudan Northeast Africa, is extra-ordinary during any crisis or catastrophes; are an exceptional race of people and great creators to survive never conquered. And so their greatest after building the Great Pyramids about **"12,000 years ago,"** "let us make man..." Because many times the man who really can't see is not the **blind** but the man who choses not too. And when emotion is high, **logic** is low.

Then **God,** after causing the donkey to speak, opened Balaam's eyes to see the angel (Numbers 22:31). When **angels** are supposedly seen in Scripture, they usually appear in the form of human beings. Specifically as men adult males, not women or children. It is said, here's how to recognize and know you have met an angel in human form:

1. Nine signs you have met an angel in human form...

2. Angelic energy. Have you ever crossed paths with someone who seemed to radiate positivity, kindness, and selflessness?
3. Over flowing kindness
4. Intuitive empathy…
5. Natural healing presence…
6. Positive energy magnet…
7. Patience in abundance.
8. A grateful heart.[That loving feeling] Sent to strengthen and or comfort you and give you courage to do what is right
9. Protection from harm

"**Historians and Scholars**" of all nationalities truly must face the reality let us make man came from man, whose ancient ruling were often called **"ruling-gods."** God's gift to man intelligent man. Could it have been perhaps "desperate times call for desperate measures." White man's rejecting with vengeance contempt, learning of his creation regardless it being suppressed or just unbelievable for the majority, and their best interest to create **"Evolution"** coming from an **ape.**

Today British men in Parliament called **"Lord"** Barrymore so and so, is no different than black ancient ruling nations referred to as **"ruling-gods** so and so. We must learn how to go with the facts and connect. America's platform is come to America "white brothers and sisters" to the land of the free and **"superior white man and woman"** not meant for inferior Black man or Latino; the 2024 election of Trump has surely shown you that as far as that goes for equality; if nothing else perhaps, no longer Democracy. If asked his excuse for such corruption could answer **"the devil made me do it,"** when he's **Satan himself!!!** But now, it's Trump's "White Nationalist – Fascism," **autocracy** (government by one person having **unlimited** power). **In America!!!** Means for now, white man's time is up to rule world-wide. With a short extension his plans **go-bust** all the way.

There's no mistake about it, perhaps the **Illuminati** had a hand in elections 2016 & 2024 out-come.

There seems **raised eyebrows** when white people hear the words let us make man, why should they this suspicious look because of what? What did blacks find out that was hidden by whites about themselves in classroom education? Theosophy (belief about God and the world held to be based on mystical insight) developed that into a global movement with Europe and United States. Colonizers [vicious conquerors] were acting as an alternative channel of intellectual exchange to colonial network [like an alternative to truth of wrong making it right], who try to popularize [or justify] their ideas among the public has failed.

1. Met with skepticism and a repelling effect to believe in. Theosophy became popular only to political activist and English-educated elites. Theosophy was connected to European Masonry, Spiritualism, Nationalist Christianity [KKK – Kuo, Klux, Klan], and had convert to black man's Hebrew, a occult "secret knowledge" connected to esoteric (Private, Secret) Masonic communities Freemasonry was a protagonist (principle character, leader of a cause) orientation. White man's aim seems was historicallizing alternative origin myths for Islam. To confuse the perception and interpretation of religious traditions by all black and brown laypeople. The rise of Islam spread within a century was over half the earth, a most amazing event in human history.

****

CHAPTER 2
The Awareness of Let Us Make Man

To correct the record, battle tested more than any other race on this planet U.S.A. white man's bottom of the list is the black man, Nubian American. Believe in black man Nubian Americans leaders of heart, with common-sense, to deliver their **politics** with **soul** logic for "we the people" to success; is research knowledge and all that's good under God to save America. In these worst of trying times formula whites always depend on **"us"** not **Latinos** nor any other race but "black."

The excuse that seems to be for putting black people down; with bias-hate, fascist-racism, and a systematic genocide is understood only by those white people who reject God's rules of His laws with their far **"superior-man"** attitude; towards an inferior supposed savage is profound resentment that claims creating of them. All nations and their nationalities regardless, comes from one, and only one **Africa** again, they resent **"let us make man."** Black and brown didn't think of or why so much animosity and undercover hate was direct towards them, not what we thought, now we **know** perhaps, now why.

Hoping to save lives with **truth** here, at that time said, "Let us make man" by a "man-god" of a nation of people, there were only black, brown, and yellow men **Acts 17:26.** Who became more increasingly wicked, corrupt in their doings and ways such as in trade, law, and belief in God that Almighty God allowed the more righteous to prophesize; well into their future; it is believed to point-out the good and the evil up to 25 thousand years ahead, it is said. And after man-god's creation of another mankind to rule for 6,000 years of the worst of hardships and wickedness (recently whose time is up). Will leave evil devious ways, and return to Him, Almighty God. Because, the wages of sin is death. When the return of the son of man (Christ), Nubian "Messiah" without any doubt that God is **God**, will be a promised by Him God, a thousand years of world **peace**. White man's, tricknology can't dispute, with changes to the KJV of the Bible.

You be the judge whether there was a "selective graftation-breeding through a certain time frame," odds of migration tribal graftation having no chance through time or the evolution of "the Caucasian race coming from an Ape," he claims. Sounds like a same likeliness of truth, which brings us to the question perhaps of what is the **"Illuminati???** Hence the genetics of the white man can only produce white will be discussed in more detail in the next chapter.

"Here is the wisdom." As prophesized, Trump is doing his job with lies and murder if you want peace prepare for war... This time surprisingly **regardless** seems, **"The Black Man Love's his child he created."** Draws a line under GOD Almighty with respect to all others if nothing else. The **child** should let no one dishonor to do harm to thy mother nor father or your days will be short GOD gave you upon earth. The creation of the white man was by the black man, the Nubian/Ethiopian Biblical Cush is **world's first civilization** on earth and was not by **Satan** the Jew, the **Devil** white man, or **Lucifer** the rebel **Satan** is **against** to the **destruction** all black and brown civilizations **"12 Tribes of Israel."** He's trying to beat the prophecy with the extension, until the coming of the Messiah, with the **triple-cross** in his last days of the 6,000 years he had to rule the world because all of GOD's little children are **innocent** until taught **"hate with racism."**

If anything the created white man's **worst enemy** is not the obvious to blame black man; but his co-beneficial in corruption and greed in sin said Biblical **Satan-Jew,** "not" created by man who says he is a Jew and is not a Jew but a liar, the **father of lies and a murderer.** Who will soon know a hard head makes a sore **"ass"** the return of the Messiah with, V.P. Harris's betterments she laid-out running for the presidency.

It is said the **"Illuminati"** is a most powerful and savagely guarded organization that secretly controls the entire modern world perhaps wearing their cloaks. It has done this mainly through being the world's **wealthiest** of people's infiltration of the **media** and **brainwashing** ruling even at this moment. It is known as one of the world's most persistent conspiracy theories on the 1969 moon landings, John F Kennedy's assassination, and 9/11, which limit themselves with regards to space and time, Illuminati enthusiasts believe that something is up with everything is very hard to disprove.

It is believed the Illuminati theoretically has existed since the dawn of time. Its insignia can be seen on the pyramids and its influence was evident around the life of black Christ. However, dating from an era before the white man existed a belief that often comes with rather unpleasant fake Euro-Jew underpinning alternate lies. It wants nothing less than to establish a **"new world order"** to which an authoritarian ruthless gang of elites would rule, and nation states be banished. A writer Kerry Thornley, who had written a jokey text on the Illuminati, decided the world was becoming too authoritarian but one way to shake that up is to get people to start questioning what they read. In time he saw how religion had **improved** his live. How respecting others and being honest made him happier.

I the author of this book just want to express his genuine feeling of just a <u>worst</u> feeling I cried tears, at eighty-three years old seeing, for little helpless black, brown, white, and Jewish children with their beautiful little smiles perhaps in pain with <u>cancer,</u> 1 in 5 will <u>die</u> at St. Jude Hospitals almost is the feeling; seeing democracy to build our nation slowly slipping away what we built with our different bloods, sweat, and tears to autocrats tearing us apart with foolish hate; is so shocking almost to believe!!! Is only Trump's personal cowards, **"stay out of prison-card!"**

We have no time to waste. At this time for our democracy, he wants to reassure us that there will be no letup from them there at the **Guardian.** He's hoping today you can help protect the **free press.** Because in his victory speech, Donald Trump called journalism **"the enemy camp."** Intimidating words. But we believe as journalists, we can't afford to be intimidated. We have a duty to tell the truth about the man the United States has just elected as president, and here at the Guardian, our reporting teams are already preparing to do the vital work of holding the incoming Trump administration to account with fearless, principled journalism. [We can be disagreeable but stand together for what's right, is what we also advocate in this book].

We the **"Guardian"** care deeply about accuracy – and our journalism is always fact-based and rigorous – but unlike many news outlets, we are open about our values and refuse to normalize authoritarianism.

We will fearlessly investigate president-elect Trump or any government official who abuses **t**heir position for personal profit or power. We will not be distracted by Washington gossip, but will stay focused on the actions and policies of the new administration. Just like your devotion to your craft the Guardian, the author of this book must interject with due respect… My objective is to point-out things of interest in history and give an analysis why things happened the way they did; with a valid point to be recognized as **fact – proven** of **truth,** with **evidence,** not speculation, that can't be disputed, and can stand-up to **"scrutiny."** And if speculative, is dutifully explained. ALERT…Stay on top our children's **"school-learning of history,"** <u>Satan</u> is changing with <u>racist,</u> <u>whitewashing</u> <u>lies!</u>

As always, the Guardian's trustworthy, principled reporting will be open to all. All around us in the US media landscape, paywalls continue to go up – but in a digital environment awash in conspiracy and disinformation, we believe access to **accurate** news about our country and world is a right for all Americans. The following is not the Guardian.

This is the countdown to world war three **"13 BLOODLINES OF THE ILLUMINATI."** One such Illuminati person David Rockefeller was the Chairman of the Council of Foreign Relations. David Rockefeller stated, "This present window of opportunity, during which a truly peaceful and independent world order might be built, will not be open for too long, we are on the verge of a global transformation. All we need is the right major crisis and the nations will accept the new world order." Rockefeller was speaking at the UN Sept. 14, 1994. The 911 attacks were the fulfillment of David Rockefeller's 1994 proclamation…

"There is no such thing in America as an independent press…We are the tools and vassals for rich men behind the scenes…Our talents, our possibilities and our lives are all the property of other men. We are intellectual prostitutes." Sources: John Swinton, former New York Times Chief of Staff.

President George H. Bush is another person of the Illuminati, who called for a New World Order called for a New World Order back in 1990. President Bush said it's the dream of the United Nation's Founders (the owners of the Council on Foreign Relations) dominate and control the world…"We have before us the opportunity to forge for ourselves and for future generations a New World Order. A world where the rule of law not the law of the **jungle** [black man's written Biblical GOD's, LAW'S], governs the conduct of nations. When we are successful, and we will be, we have a real chance at this New World Order. An order in which a credible United Nations can use a peace-keeping role, to fulfil the promise and vision of the UN's founders." President George H. Bush, 1990.

Isn't it amazing how the United Nations causes most of the war and bloodshed around the globe, while continually their talking about peace. They're always willing to have peace, even if it means going to war, and they often do! Isaiah 48:22, "There is no peace, saith the LORD, unto the wicked." This sinful world will never have peace until the King of Kings return, Jesus Christ, and destroys the New

World Order and casts its members into Hell.

"The real rulers in Washington are **invisible,** and exercise power from behind the scenes." Supreme Court Judge Felix Frankfurter.

The era of the New World Order has begun, beginning with the 911 attacks. William Guy Carr tried to warn us 60-years ago, in his eye-opening book, <u>Pawns In The Game</u>, but so few people cared enough to listen. 2nd Thessalonians 2:10 tells us that the masses of this world will eagerly follow the <u>Antichrist</u> because, "they received not the **love** of the **truth** that they might be **saved.**"

The average American is woefully ignorant, which as you've read as far as Mr. Rockefeller is concerned. There is no greater weapon used against the common man than to keep him **ignorant.** Eve sinned in Genesis 3:6 out of ignorance. The Bible says she was deceived, for had she known **THE TRUTH** she would not eaten of the forbidden. Biblical Eve, just like the American public today believed a **"LIE."** The average American especially white-supremacy theorist, is still mad at black and brown Muslims over the 911 attacks, while the real culprits have us eating out of their hands while perhaps sacrificing 911.

It's a big lie in our churches that we must **support** Israel. It's called the heresy of <u>Zionism</u>. The Lord promised in the Old Testament to **Regather Israel** to her Promised Land when he returns at the second coming. This is a Fake-Euro Jew heated and controversial subject, but we should be tired of pastors telling people to financially support Godless, Christ-rejecting, blasphemous and wicked people simply because they live in Israel. The main reason Euro-Fake Jew **Boards of American Education;** always begin black man history with the false impression of starting in **Egypt;** instead of spoken 58 times in the Bible, the **Nubian/Ethiopian Cush,** Sahara Sudan represents black skinned Jesus Christ of <u>Judah's Israel</u>; ancient African's Continent TRUE History beginning of **civilization itself.** They lie to substantiate their false fake-Jew Israeli-nation.

We say all of the above to say this, now president elected Trump is making America's image to black and brown people world-wide look like the **"land of Satan."** Just like fake-Jew racist

Israeli's, are to Palestinians. The nomad Euro-Fake Jew, has no history building a country or nation of their own; they infiltrate and excel in others to take over which causes problems and trouble. As a start to prove the point, in 1492 AD they were run-out of Spain by Queen Isabella in trying to take over trouble-makers.

We all know through history "the horrible lesson of extermination" the fake-Jew went through in Germany caused a world war of Euro-**Caucasian** against Euro-**Jew**. For centuries the Jew is attached to the number 6 million lives. At the time of the death camps of Germany, at the top the most Jews in Germany was 250,000 because many had fled and not 6 million lost. Is the lie number they have used through the centuries is, **"6 Million Jews."** So why didn't President Truman in 1948 give Euro-Jews 60% of a land to build a nation in **Europe;** instead of **non-aggressive** Africa's already settled homeland, so-called by white's waste-land of Israel. And the trouble maker has caused **wars and rumors of wars** ever since! The Euro-Jew has never been one of **"The 12 Tribes of Israel."** By CONVERTING to the original black Hebrew religion the fake-Jew lies making it appear originated by him with false white depictions of him.

This is not anti-Semitic talk, because the hypocritical Euro-Jew are anti-black Hebrew. Every time a Jew use the expression anti-Semitic behind black people exposing them, insults the dignity, integrity and pride of black people tired of its racist undertones; every time Euro-Jews use the expression anti-Semitic.

The sad truth of all the above is when you realize, there has never been accepted in America, nor elected a **"JEW"** president. Perhaps seems to reason why, close but not winning the election a **black** Asian American **woman** married to a JEW lost the 2024 election for president of these United States, would rather accepted a male aristocrat than a woman, black, Jew-lover. And with all the betterments for the middle-class working people Vice president

Harris proposed, still America elected Trump for the wealthy president. All the good and positive structures we were taught to believe in, we will soon see fall apart with Trump so sad. However, we will summon our spirit and relentlessly **fight** bravely what we now gain letting nothing slip-away again.

Remember, the gift to man a medicine is **"MUSIC."** The joy of music is **godly,** its cultures red, yellow, black, brown, white, bring us together in peace. Is the one thing "poison of hate" can never conquer its love like sunshine, music cleanses the soul. It will be sunshine from darkness when the "song of democracy" rain in America once more by the deafening sound of the bugle-call to "war music march to the death." In drum beat, we the people especially Nubian Americans again for democracy will struggle with fight and will win; and the after new nor old soldiers who fought will never die or be forgotten; but slowly one by one bravely with GOD just forever fade away...

We need to represent each other. In 1950, 200,000 Jewish immigrants interred America through the boarder, between Mexico and the US just as thousands of needy men, women, children, and babies of black and brown peoples. Whether it's accepted or not people all over the world must realize, taught, and learn we somehow "one big family," respectfully began with the essence of blackness the beginning and the end, Alfa and Omega. And now elected president Trump. He is spitting in your face telling you its only rain. But what you sow, so shall you reap. There are no exception to this rule proven through history. We are all immigrants to the Native Americans. With the exception of the Nubian American <u>ex</u>-<u>slave</u> brought here against his will on <u>depraved</u> slave-ships. Can you imagine the joy of Almighty God, when His world finally comes together back to Him, by its own choice.

What the Illuminati is trying do, it wants to establish a new world order which an authoritarian gang of elites would rule, under which nation states would be banished. Alternately, it is part of a fight against so-called fake news, which began in the 1960s. A journalist for

Playboy magazine called along with a writer Kerry Thornley, who had written a jokey text on the Illuminati, decided that the world was becoming too authoritarian, and one way to shake that up would be to get people to start questioning what they read cannot be said enough.

Just like truth of the Illuminati to "The Ancient Aliens Origins Lies: History Channel. One subject is, the mystery how the black man built the great pyramids envied by the white man has actually said, "couldn't have come about on our own," what the black man actually did **on his own!** And the black man being Nubian of the Sudan, were **great Seafarers** exchanged knowledge with scattered ancient biblical "12 tribes of Israel" in the South Americas, building pyramids with high-technology, exchanged other important things of technology even flight and surprisingly nuclear forms of technology.

The white man is "Johnny come lately" without a history seeing black and brown men in flying-ships he's gonna call to spite, "Aliens" coming from another world instead of reporting without speculation or his stupid opinion, only the fact of what he saw. Just can't be the black man with such intelligence's to create with high advanced technology is coming from the mouth of hypocritical great liar of history white man. This is not hate talk, it is TRUTH talk with facts and proof/evidence. Making it all look like "alien-tech," until it comes to ancient white Greeks or Romans.

It's almost like only what comes out the mouth (like a prayer book) of the white man decide to say is to be believed the truth and not what you see is why white men would chip-away the thick nose and lips recognized as black to discourage identity. Such as the Great Sphinx of Egypt and black sculptor's artifacts and whitewash black Egyptian paintings the interior of the great pyramids. Like we blacks need him the white man having no history to teach us, needs him to know about ours, he hides or distorts as his in disguise. Wow.

His technical aliens are only black and brown people of earth called gods of high-advanced technology of this planet, even nuclear energy because it is said many times "There's Nothing New Under the Sun;" and they the white man hides the vital fact the Sudan **Nubian** Civilization is before the **Sumerian** Civilization the white man lies about; not spoken of in whiteman's text books of schooling, why??? And the lie the Sumerians being the first civilization all the while knowing it was the Nubian all put together is a message the white man is trying to get-around the time-frame truth of **"Let Us Make Man"** or he wouldn't have had **Sudan's** history AVOIDED!

From a **"great history,"** today is a world-wide EMERGANCY do the right thing to help; stop the mass suffering in the Nubian **SUDAN** of Africa, where **26 million** people are threaten with famine with an on-going civil-war; equals ½ of all the world's hardship, misery. The Sudan population of their people and their children as **human beings** are not built like anyone else's, woman to with-stand this cruelty for long, facing only death. Please do your share with a "humanity-action," against a civil-war to help change their lives to just survive to live!!!   Historians of all nationalities, truly must face the reality, let us make man came from man's ancient ruling as gods, that God intended making it clear beforehand man would recognize, it not being Him talking to angels.

And not controversy whether certain scripter meanings has been changed, in the KJV Bible by devious white-scholars to fit their aim, perhaps with confusion for all mankind. However, now here is Yacub's clear scientific FACT creation of an unusual type of man. While the now created white man needs a valid excuse for his creating a history, incorrect with **evolution.** There is none, but he made a complete turn-around from **ape** to "Ancient Alien creatures" from another world that all white scholars agree with on national TV; with possible genetics to deceive himself seeming valid against, let us make man coming from the **"black man."**

"Echoes of Mr. Yakub after Patmos," by Tingba Muhammad, a guest columnist. The human breeding process that created the White race has now been corroborated by scientists of the University of

Copenhagen who show that a major genetic bifurcation (to divide into two branches or parts) occurred at the EXACT time The Most Honorable Elijah Muhammad said it did, 6,000 years ago, when they say all blue-eyed humans can point a single parent.

The breeding of animals and plants to create hybrid enhancements is a process that had been used in farming and animal husbandry for centuries [even] before Mr. Yakub adapted it to human beings for his calculated objective. And just as a farmer must isolate the animals he is breeding to ensure the purity of his final product, Mr. Yakub also needed isolation in the form of an island laboratory to secure his 600-year human breeding experiment. He chose the island of Patmos in the Aegean Sea, about 36 miles from the coast of Turkey, because it was relatively invulnerable to outside interference and genetic contamination.

And once Yakub's 600-year "made man" entered the world, all of history took a devastating turn. Early signs of this were evident with the ancient Egyptians, who worried about a strange tribe of blue-eyed people they called **Tamahu** – "the created ones" – a clear allusion to their unnatural origins. The Tamahu moved onto the edge of the desert and demonstrated a proclivity for trouble-making, foreshadowing a troubling modus operandi (a method of procedure).

By his own written record we can trace the movements of this created man around the globe as he ultimately subdued every nation, race, and people with whom he came in contact. By 1890 a United States senator could portentously report to the President that "the race to which we belong is the most arrogant and rapacious, the most exclusive and indomitable in history. It is the conquering and the unconquerable race, through which alone man has taken possession of the physical and moral world. ...All other races have been its enemies or its victims."

Overlooked in our view of history is a crucial part of the Caucasian's methodology of conquest that was adopted directly from the knowledge they gained on Patmos Island. The Messenger said that Yacub lived for 150 years but that, "He gave his people guidance in the form of literature" on "What they should do and ... how to rule the black nation." A review of history shows Yacub's created man continued to follow Yacub's methodology and directions long into the future.

We can actually see this in the Caucasian's repeated use of isolated islands as laboratories to breed or create a people for designated functions in European colonization schemes. [Like the Mulatto]. In fact, some of the strongest proof of Yacub's very existence is the fact that his genetic breeding experiments on Patmos have been replicated so often and so successfully. The need to create a lighter-skinned substitute ruler over the earth's indigenous peoples seems to have been the purpose of these colonial experiments. The results shown the physical features and biological immunities to the diseases of the indigenous people. His mentality and actions would reflect the aims and desires of his European creator. Tracing the Jewish history of expansion out of Europe provides more than a few examples of the island laboratories that echo this Yakubian technique.

In the mid-1400s, Portuguese King Dom Manuel colonized the African coastal islands of Sao Tome and Principle in order "to whiten the race," as he put it. Two thousand [Euro] Jews and their children, as well as their orphans, went to those African islands specifically for that "whitening" purpose. They became masters of the sugar trade and developed the slavery-intensive model for the plantation economy that would soon thereafter dominate the Western Hemisphere for the coming centuries. On these two islands alone the Euro-Jewish sugar planters imported and enslaved 3,000 Africans.

About that same time [Euro] Jewish slave merchants from Portugal invaded the Cape Verde islands, about 350 miles off the coast of Senegal Africa. They kidnapped and raped black women, and the mixed-race progeny, called **Lancados,** were sent into the African mainland for the express purpose of trading in Black human beings. White historians hide these malevolent half-breeds under the name

"Africans" when whites lie, claiming that "Africans sold each other." So brazen were these pushed into life or death situations by whites, light-skinned newcomers that they even were implanted in the local population as "African chiefs."

The Euro-Jewish thinking on this very issue was **revealed** by Rabbi Dr. Louis M. Epetein, in his book Sex Laws and Customs in **Judaism:** "The female slave was a sex tool beneath the level of moral consideration by the white man [but was **against her-will**]. She was an economic good, useful, in addition to her menial labor, for breeding more slaves. To attain that purpose, the master mated her [so-called white man's concern was what his woman was, he made it a black woman] was promiscuously according to his breeding plans. The [low-life] master himself and his sons and other members of his [degenerate] household took turns with her for the increase [excuse] of the family wealth …"

[There were **"brave"** and strong **"morally"** black slave men and **stout** enduring women who planned; then swiftly **killed** plantation's hateful racist and degenerate white heinously evil men, which immediately after, had to flee to the north, that saved their lives of "courageous" **action!** And God bless those men and women the suffering who didn't quite make it north, forever our hat's goes off out of **"respect"** too.]

The African experience on the **French**-stolen Caribbean island of **Haiti** reflects the **Yakubian** mindset of the Caucasian. The prominent role of the mixed-race mulattos as agents of the French repression was on full display during the **Haitian Revolution** between 1792 and 1804, when the enslaved Africans rose up to defend Napoleon. Rabbi Harold Sharfman wrote that the Frenchmen were "whitening" African females for sexual purposes: "French and Spanish plantation owners in Santo Domingo Haiti, selective breeding, produced an exotic type with remarkably exquisite facial features, lithe bodies, small hands and feet. These above all were sought as mistresses.

The pillagers (thieves) that travelled with Columbus to the

islands of the West Indies in 1492 were obviously programmed in the Yakubian point of view. One of them wrote the first recorded rape in the New World: "While I was in the boat I captured a very beautiful Carib woman and I conceived desire to take pleasure ... but she did not want it and treated me with her finger nails in such a manner that I wished I had never begun. But seeing that ... I took a rope and thrashed her well, for which she raised such unheard of screams that you would not have believed your ears ..."

A shockingly similar story is found in documents from the earliest settlement of an island in the Boston harbor. In the 1630s, a shipper named Samuel Maverick enslaved more than thirty African men, women, and children at his small fortified mansion on Noddles Island (now East Boston). An English traveler recounted "Mr. Maverick was desirous to have a breed of Negroes" but that an African woman would not yield to him. Our Black sister, he reported, "had been a queen in her country." A "Maverick Square" near Boston's major airport is now named for the degenerate.

In South America we find that even when a large land mass is being colonized, the islands are still sought after by white men Caucasian settlement. A **Dutch Jew** named David Nassi created a little "Jewish homeland" on a large island in the Surinam River that became known as the "Savannah of the Jews." Soon these Jews owned vast sugar, coffee, cotton, and lumber plantations using many thousands of enslaved Africans. By 1791, there were reportedly 100 "Jewish mulattoes" – the "whitened" result of the rape of African women by Jewish slave masters.

As we can see, the island breeding method of Yakub can be observed in many societies as Europeans moved to impose their will upon the world. And just as on Patmos, this birth control plan coincided with a "strict law" and mental training to prepare the mixed-race progeny for rulership their indigenous victims. This vital acculturation process has been concealed in the history of the African slave trade under the terms "seasoning" and **"Christianizing,"** though the purpose of this **Yakubian** process had nothing to do with **Jesus** or His liberating principles. Again, islands factored strongly in this equation. Africans were warehoused in huge numbers on Barbados and Jamaica to then be distributed to regional markets. "Seasoning-camps" were prominent here and it was estimated that only one in four (1/4) Africans, could be broken down and made into reliable slaves.

In West Africa, Dutch "explorers" set up an actual school system for the mixed-race mulattos lasting two centuries! According to white-scholars, the intention was that graduates would be mentally and biologically better suited to the European system and the African climate and thus would be able to replace White Dutch officials in maintaining white <u>racist</u> <u>supremacist</u> <u>hate</u> colonial rule. One such school in **Ghana** Africa, "admitted only boys who it was hoped would become **soldiers** who would form a mulatto guard for the Danish forts on the coast." All were trained to rule over the Black world.

What we see is that since that fateful original enterprise on Patmos Island 6,600 years ago, there have been a succession of human breeding experiments on remote island laboratories---clear echoes of Yakub's original model. His purpose was to breed a human being that would not only rule but could carry out that Yakubian method through the Caucasian white man's 6,000 year reign. It took an island of isolation to perfect this unruly and unrulable product, and the clear result is "an exclusive and indomitable" man who has done exactly as The Messenger taught he was created to do---create mischief and cause the shedding of blood. And, just as The Messenger said, his time of rule has now come to an end. (Tingba Muhammad is a citizen of the Nation of Islam and a member of the NOI Research Group NOIRG.org).

Absorbing all of the above and before we give you how Yakub created the white man next first we want to go into something important to read that is so sad; with racial hate towards black people, if only meant in jest couldn't get a smile... Now with all this knowledge and evidence of history above, we now give you the white man's new famous abstract theory of a far-fetched "space aliens from another world" only to take-away credit of the black man's high-intellect of advanced-technology in science he has that's ancient; envied not having by the white man begins.

"**Religion**" – As Erich Von Daniken says it, "As humans we often look to religion to solve the mysteries of life believing that there is an all-powerful creator that loves and has given us gifts as the chosen people [black people]. We believe that we are have been given guidelines to behaviors. We are told that we should worship our creator and pledge our faith so that we will be rewarded at the end. We are told of an afterlife of comfort and joy from our creator "God." This part will focus on religion and how it could be interpreted to support the **Ancient Astronaut Hypothesis.**

This of course is explains the creation of our planet but what about mankind. The Bible addresses these issues later in Genesis; "*26 And God said, Let us make man in our image, after our likeness: and let them have dominion over the fish of the sea ...* The Sumerian's have, [just skip-over block-out Nubian/Egyptian original explanation], the "Epic of Creation" which is a tablet that describes Creation in much the same way and other things.

Science of coarse offers different theories such as evolution. Encyclopedia Britannica describes evolution as this; "*evolution, theory in biology postulating that the various types of plants, animals, and other living things on Earth have their origin in other preexisting types and that the distinguishable differences are due to modifications in successive generations.*" If this theory is correct then mankind would have evolved from lower primates rather than a Creator God. [And we know the first man, the black man, was created instantaneous by God.]

Science tells us that the building blocks of all living things are DNA. On July 5, 1996 scientists at the Roslin Institute in Midlothian,

Scotland cloned an adult sheep from a mammary cell and called her Dolly. This served as proof that a mammal could be cloned. If we can clone a sheep it's possible eventually to manipulate DNA of living things even more. If humans can manipulate DNA then it could be that humans came from manipulated DNA possible that Adam was created from building block materials on earth and then had his DNA manipulated with the DNA of God; [but you're not talking about the black man created by God in His image black man then created the Caucasian white man on Patmos island; must be only the white man came from manipulated DNA by who Yakub?]

[The Astronaut theory can't be supported by God having a DNA makes Eric Von Daniken look stupid coming out his mouth with such absurdity, just like the evolution theory; showing (always artist-drawn). The "White Man" coming from a little **"monkey,"** into an **"ape-man,"** then white man but never not the **"Black Man!"** The Black Man came from God. The white man **came** from created by the black man. And all other of mankind came from **"Africa,"** in the beginning. He hates with a passion by him distorting, whitewashing and omitting "Black Nubian/Egyptian history."]

[What is it about a "Great Nubian Civilization," the world's first, the white man intentionally wants to completely ignore in "history-education," but why? Could it be the Yakubian process is Nubian "prophecy." Why the white man won't teach or even mention in all his history books that white scholars also omits, **"Nubian"** in grammar, high-school, and higher learning. Steps to prevent this and "Nubian put into text," still has not been taken. He "fears and is ashamed" he's the **"ALIEN"** on this planet certainly he won't put that in text. It was nappy-haired Nubians said, "let us make man," the world deserves to know the facts what's going on with the **"truth,"** will set you free without insult; unalike the white man's twisted lies.]

Erich Von Daniken stated in an interview for the program *"The Mysterious World"* He believed that the earth had been visited by Ancient Astronauts and these Astronauts had manipulated human

DNA. Daniken states the proof can be found in Lexor, Egypt. He believes that the Sphinx statues were created for their Gods. Many of these Gods were Alien Astronauts and others were created by the Egyptians have many references to these Hybrid Gods. Daniken believes one possible reason for these Astronauts to do this is to create beings that could survive that could survive on planets with other temperatures. According to Erich Von Daniken these Monster Gods probably died and were buried deep within the tombs. [He can't be serious, because no such evidence of any of this has never been found, to hold-up any of this foolishness, really.]

The Chariot is not the only example of earlier humans witnessing flight. In a 2007 lecture Jason Martell an Ancient Astronaut researcher discussed the flying gods of Sumerian's and Egyptians [but of course must omit the "flying black gods of Nubians" who ruled Egypt's 25th Dynasty its greatest time of Egypt's advancement.] It's Martell's belief that these cultures depicted these gods with wings. It was their only way to describe flight. He also believes we see more examples of this in South America with the Incas. They left sample sculptures of the flight machines that they've seen according to Jason. He believes that the Incas saw these beings as Gods that came from these flying machines. [Not Gods, they were human Nubians, Egyptians, and Sumerians departing from their high-tech flying machines.]

Reminds us of today just as with the fortitude of liberty, the spectacular and energetic Nubian American as public servants will pave the way many unbeknown their duty saving **"Democracy"** again in America. Who fought for "civil-rights laws" 80 years, laws are under **"attack."** We must unite to guarantee these laws so hard fought for stay in place. With concerns of Donald Trump calling Africa ass-hole countries... Not a king nor god his ego relishes is against all the above.

Getting back to the subject, and so the African Aborigines saw World War 1 pilots as Gods. The servicemen/Gods could eat without hunting and never ran out of food. When the servicemen left, the natives created model planes and air strips in hopes of their gods returning [or perhaps were still used not explained.] Of coarse flight is not the only technology that may have been described by religion. It is also possible that religion describes ["let us make man"] and weapons of mass destruction. This is present in the Indian culture as well as *"the Bible."*

Ancient Indian texts known as *"the Mahabharatra"* discuss the Vimana. It's described as a flying vessel heavily armed and used by the Gods to wage war. According to Indian lore the crafts were armed with energy and projectile weapons. One battle puts the hero known as Krishna in pursuit of his enemy Salva. During the battle Krishna fires a special weapon of sound to destroy. Later in *"the Mahabharatra"* the Vimana deploy a great thunderbolt weapon against three cities. Check out this telling of that event;

"Gurkha flying in his swift and powerful Vimana hurled against the three cities of the Vrishis and Andhakas a single projectile charged with the all the power of the Universe. An incandescent column of smoke and fire, as brilliant as ten thousands suns, rose in all its splendour. It was the unknown weapon, the Iron Thunderbolt, a gigantic messenger of death which reduced to ashes the entire race of the Vrishnis and Andhakas." "The Mahabharatra." This is type weapon could also be mentioned in *"the Bible."* "24 Then the LORD rained upon Sodom and upon Gomorrah brimstone and fire from the LORD out of heaven; 25 And he overthrew those cities, and all the plain, and all the inhabitants of the cities, and that which grew upon the ground. 26 But his wife looked back from behind him, and she became a pillar of salt. 27 And Abraham gat up early in the morning…

Both religious texts sound as very similar to the destruction caused by the atomic bomb. It seems that both texts describe the result to appear as burned area. There are also descriptions of total loss of life. [There is nothing new under the sun bares truth here and reminds us later on in history the white man dropping on the yellow man twice atomic bombs to early end the war but won't drop no atomic bomb in white man's Europe, to save lives and earlier end the war!]

There are other examples of science and technology particularly in things that were given to man. The Sumerians and Egyptians [and of course the exceptional **Nubians** are always left out of history, by the hateful envious white man because of Nubian, let us make white man] serve as examples of societies with knowledge beyond their time.

[The Nubian/Egyptian and] the Sumerians had great knowledge of astrology. They could identify planets and constellations. The interesting thing is that they referred to Earth as the seventh planet instead of the third. This is because they were counting from the other direction. It could be possible that they were receiving this information from travelers coming into our solar system. [Or a Daniken's fantasy creation]. There are several problems with the Ancient Astronaut Hypothesis. The first is interpretation. Then the lack of hard evidence becomes the issue. The final issue is expert credibility.

Daniken implies the assertion that intelligence of our earliest ancestors began a million years ago developed in communities does not hold water. In terms of the history or evolution leap from animalistic being to homo-sapiens took place overnight. A miracle? Miracles just don't happen. [But what white man Daniken doesn't realize having no belief, that "GOD is the Absolute Miracle" of our universe!!!] I am trying to produce arguments for my conviction that in the very beginning there was only one source of the origin of homo-sapiens, namely the spaceman who first made the mutation (an inherited physical or biochemical change in genetic material). [Is Daniken saying, the black man being the first homo-sapiens was the spaceman who made the mutation of the white man, let us make man, and if so, what type of mutation is Daniken talking about; unless the white man is a mutation, he's saying really doesn't make sense like all of what he's saying!]

Only much later, when peoples and races had settled in other parts of the globe, were new experiments in new places introduced into the first primordial tradition. But the core of the act of creation, namely that the gods created the first men in their own images, is preserved in all the world-wide traditions! The creation of man by extraterrestrial intervention does not interfere with the theory of our ancestry or the theory of evolution. By Erich Von Daniken "The Gold of the Gods" – Let us make man in our image, after our likeness, and let them have dominion over the fish of the sea, and over the fowl of the air …" (Genesis 1:26).

The information available makes the believable, but not provable. There are several experts who have great arguments but none can provide 100%. I'm willing to believe it's possible. I'm not willing to call it fact. James Hisum, did a tour of duty in the 82nd Airborne Division of the U.S. Army had an interest in the Alien Astronaut Theory.

****

CHAPTER 3
Yacub's Scientific Creation of Man

Now, **"Let Us Make Man"** Genesis 1:26 – Then God said, "Let us make man in our image, after our likeness. And let them have dominion over the fish of the sea, and over the birds of the heavens, and over the livestock, and over every creeping thing that creeps on the earth;" Rev. 1:9, and 3:13-14. John was there exiled to Patmos, by order of the emperor Domitian, the most powerful man on Earth, of his time. John not only received a strong message for the Seven Isles (the 7 churches) that he pastored and even would pastor, but he saw the **"prophecy of the future,"** the world of the end of a time – The coming of Christ, the final judgment.

Genesis 1:26 – Why Does the Bible Use the Plural "Us" When God Refers to Himself? Problem: Orthodox Christian and Jewish scholars maintain that God is one. In fact, the historic confession of the faith of Israel is taken from Deuteronomy 6:4 which says, "Hear, O Israel: The Lord our God, The Lord is one!" However, if God is one why does this verse in Genesis use the word "Us?"

Solution: Several explanations throughout history offered. Some commentators [Europeans] have claimed that this is merely a case where God is addressing the angles. But verse 27 makes it clear that God [a man god prophet John, scientist Yakub] created [European] man in *His own [black]* image; in the image of *God"* and NOT in the image of the angles of the Christian **Holy Bible** King James Version **"and"** the Islamic Bible the **Holy Koran.**

In order for something incredible! Like cutting off the head of the serpent, the snake! We respectfully here get annoyed with European history, omitting Nubian history and direct truth "honoring their parents" but perhaps not how exactly the method; but how they came into this world as a people created by man, prophesized, and carried out in history by the black man. Islam didn't hold back no-punches explaining with direct facts, how, why, when, where, and the results with proof/evidence of the white man. Scientist Yakub the same man prophet John on Patmos Island made white people whereas white man's true creation is hidden in Christianity won't tell. But the white man is "quick" to say a lie; so wrong that the black man came from a white **Libyan** tribe in Africa. They hate that the world's first culture of civilization was the Nubian/Ethiopian black man so much as to pathetically try to only, artist drawn so-called evidence, coming from a monkey, to an ape man type, then white man's **evolution!** He needs to be ashamed of himself... I'd rather know the bitter **truth** than the sweet lie of history!!!

Special thanks is for the writing here, is given to Jason F McDonald jfmcdo00@mik.uky.edu Subject: Re: black mans historypt (long) /** Speech delivered by Malcom X while he was still with the Nation of Islam – Black Man's History.

The following is from the late renowned Islamic Minister and Black Prince of his people Malcolm X, relaying the message of the Honorable Elijah Muhammad. Dec. 1962, **"Black Man's History"** by Malcolm X explains: Black or White no one can give biological evidence to show that Black is the stronger or superior of the two if you want to make that kind of comparison. [We here always have to take in account those who can't reason or comprehend as well as us, like the following. Don't throw stones white man, then hide your head what atrocities you did behind a white man is superior hoax!]

[White man, please answer these 3 questions with honesty first because the truth come out next. One, what have you done in political black man's history? Two, What did you do it for? Three, what have you done in history white man? Absolutely nothing but war! There are many guardrails and guidelines in America, but they are NOT **"written"** in LAW. Democracy's job is to "up-hold the rule of law;" whereas, only **"facts"** matter. Trump is dismantling the rule of law creating a burning anger amongst poor people's helplessness to a corrupt new system that's taking the advantage of healthcare. Who tried to get his own vice president killed! A miss-character and wrong depictions is a negative whelm; politics supported by an **"Artistic License law"** is to get-over on black & brown people's education, jeopardizing their learning experience as **fray** (FIGHT), STRUGGLE; also: QUARREL, DISPUTE, IRRITATE). With no **legal** recourse!!! Trumpism, a 34 count felon, of his second term in only six weeks saying he would be a dictator his first day in office 2025, is destroying America's checks and balances is dangerous to just survive much less living any more, must end with removal some way, some way how, right now!

Before we get into the profound speech Malcolm X gave of "let us make man," first we'll begin with his speech of Dec. 1962, "Black Man's History." And before we start, we here want to say, "We love and respect the **"good"** in all nationalities;" only the bad in all we worry about, but none too much, is with true and correct black, brown and white man's history; the best we could research to give, a deserving you to know the whole truth. There was a black man's great **"Prehistory,"** who ruled the world before white man history, a must to be told, to **"Inspire!!!"**]

Minister Malcom X says, I want to thank Allah [God] for coming and giving to us our leader and teacher here in America, the Honorable Elijah Muhammad… Today dark mankind is waking up and is under taking a new type of thinking that is creating new approaches and new reactions that make it almost impossible to figure out what the black man is going to do next, and by black man we mean as we are taught by the Honorable Elijah Muhammad we include all those who are nonwhite. He teaches us that black is the basic color that black is the foundation or the basic of all colors… We don't separate our color from our religion. The white man doesn't.

The white man never has separated Christianity from white, nor has he separate the white man from Christianity. When you hear the white man bragging, "I'm a Christian," he's bragging about being a white man. ...I used to hear them [parents] when I was a little child sing the song "Wash Me White as Snow." My father was a black man and my mother was a black woman, but yet the songs that they sang in their church were designed to fill their hearts with the desire to be white. So many people, especially our people get resentful when they hear me say something like this. But rather than get resentful all they have to do is think back on many of the songs and much of the teachings and the doctrines that they were taught while they were going to church and they'll have to agree that it was all designed to make us look down on black and up on white.

The religion that the Honorable Elijah Muhammad is teaching us here in America today, is designed to undo in our minds what the white man what the white man has done to us. It's designed to undo the type of brainwashing that we have had to undergo for four hundred years at the hands of the white man in order to bring us down to the level that we are today. So when you hear us often refer to black in almost a boastful way, actually we're not boasting, what we're doing is telling the truth about our people... So never think ill...if an overemphasis seems to be placed on the word black, but rather sit and analyze and try to get an understanding.

You have to have a knowledge of history no matter what you are going to do; anything that you undertake you have to have a knowledge of history [self]in order to be successful in it. ...There are black people in America who have mastered the mathematical sciences, have become professors and experts in physics, are able to toss sputniks out there in the atmosphere, out in space. They are masters in that field. We have black men who have mastered the field of medicine, we have black men who have mastered other fields, but very seldom do we have black men in America who have mastered the knowledge of the history of the black man himself. We have among our people those who are experts in every field, but seldom can you find one among us who is an expert on the history of the black man.

I might stop right here to point out that some of you may say, "I came up here to listen to some religion about Islam, but now all I hear you talk about is black." We don't separate our color from our religion. The white man doesn't. The white man never has separated Christianity from white, nor has he separated the white man from Christianity. When you hear the white man bragging, "I'm a Christian," he's bragging about being a white man. Then you have the Negro. When he is bragging about being a Christian, he's bragging about [washing his sins away unbeknowning…] he's a white man, or wants to be white… My mother was a Christian and my father was a Christian and I use to hear them when I was a child sing the song "Wash Me White as Snow."

So many people, get resentful when they hear me say this but…think back on many of the songs and much of the teachings and the doctrines they were taught while they were going to church and they'll have to agree that it was all designed to make us look down on black and up on white. So the religion that we have, the religion of Islam, the religion that makes us Muslims, the religion that the Honorable Elijah Muhammad is teaching us here in America today, is designed to undo in our minds what the white man has done to us.

There are black people in America who have mastered the mathematical sciences, have become professors and experts in physics are able to toss sputniks out there in the atmosphere, out in space. They are masters in that field. We have black men who have mastered other fields, but very seldom do we have black men in America who have mastered the knowledge of the history of the black man himself…

And because of his lack of knowledge concerning the history of the black man , no matter how much he excels in the other sciences, he's always confined, he is always relegated to the same low rung of the ladder that the dumbest of our people are relegated to. And all of this stems from his lack of knowledge concerning history. What made Dr. George Washington Carver a Negro scientist instead of a scientist? What made Paul Robeson a Negro actor instead of an actor? What made, or makes Ralph Bunche a Negro statesman and instead of a statesman? The only difference between Bunche and Caver and these others I just mentioned is they don't know the history of the black man. Bunche is an expert, and international politician, but he doesn't know himself, he doesn't know the history of the black people. He can be sent all over the world by America to solve problems for America, or to solve problems for other nations, but he can't solve problems for his own people in this country. Why? What is it that ties our people up in this way? The Honorable Elijah Muhammed says that it boils down to just one word-history.

When you study the history of Bunche, his history is different from the history of the black man who just came here from Africa. And if you notice, when Bunche was in Atlanta, Georgia, during the summer of the NAACP Convention, he was Jim Crowed, he was segregated, he was not allowed to go in a hotel down there. Yet there are Africans who came here, black as night, who can go into those cracker hotels. Well, what is the difference between Bunche and one of them? The difference is Bunche doesn't know his history, and they, the Africans, do know their history. They may come here out of the jungles, but they know their history. They may come here wearing sheets with their heads all wrapped up, but they know their history. You and I can come out of Harvard but we don't know our history. There's a basic difference in why we are treated as we are: one knows his history and one doesn't know his history! The American so-called Negro is a soldier who doesn't know his history; he's a servant who doesn't know his history; he's a graduate of Columbia, or Yale, or Harvard, or Tuskegee, who doesn't know his history. He's confined, he's limited, he's held under the control and the jurisdiction of the white man who knows more about the history of the Negro than the Negro knows about himself. But when you and I wake up, as we're taught by the Honorable Elijah Muhammad, and learn our history, learn the history of our kind, then the white man will be at a disadvantage and we'll be at an advantage.

The only thing that puts you and me at a disadvantage is our lack of knowledge concerning history. So one of the reasons, one of the missions, one of the objectives of the Honorable Elijah Muhammad here in America is to only to teach you and me the right religions but to teach you and me history. In fact, do you know that if you and I know history we know the right religion? The only way that you can become confused, that you can become mixed up and not know which religion belongs to God, is if you don't know history. In fact, you have to know history to know something about God. You have to know history to know something about God's religion. You have to know history to know something about God's people. You have to know history to know something about God's plans and God's purposes, and, as I say, the only people who don't know history are the American so-called Negroes. If you know history, for example, you know when you look at this religion right here [writes "Christianity" on the black board] the only way you can explain it is to have knowledge of history.

Why is it called Christianity? It is called Christianity, they say, because it was named after a man called Christ who was born two thousand years ago. Now you know, brothers and sisters, God is an old God, and the world is an old world. The universe has been here a long time. I think all of you would agree that the universe has been here longer than two thousand years. Then you'll also agree that the universe was made by God himself, that God created the universe. God created the people who are on this earth, God wouldn't create a universe, God wouldn't set a thing up in the sky that makes nine planets rotate around it, all of them inhabited, you and I inhabiting the planet earth upon which we live-God wouldn't have done all of this and not given people a religion. God put His religion here at the creation of the universe. Now then, since you agree to this and you'll agree also that Christ was born two thousand years ago, this couldn't have been God's religion. Your knowledge of history tells you that God couldn't call His religion Christianity because Christianity is only two thousand years old. So if this is the case, then what was God's religion called before the birth of Christ? Can you see the importance of history? Why, if you didn't know history you'd think that Christianity was God's religion, and you'd be running around here wondering why everybody doesn't practice it. Because some people have a better knowledge of history than others do, it is only the people whose knowledge of history is limited who jump up and say that Christianity is the name of God's religion. If Christianity hasn't always been the name of God's religion it isn't now the name of God's religion. God doesn't change his mind; God's mind is made up from the beginning. He doesn't have to change his mind because He knows all there is to know all the way down the wheel of time. He never has to change His mind, His mind is made up, His knowledge is complete, all encompassing. Do you understand? So once you can see, and I think you can, then it's almost impossible for God to call Christianity His religion.

What should God call His religion? Christians are the ones who call God's religion Christianity, but God was here before Christians came on the scene. They tell you that Christians began back there with the Romans, with one of the Roman Emperors who accepted the teachings of some of Jesus' disciples and then named what the disciples taught "Christianity." But Jesus didn't call it Christianity, it wasn't named until two or three hundred years after Jesus was dead. Right or wrong? Any history book will tell you this, any theologian knows this, and the only Negroes who will contend this are those who don't know history, and most Negroes will contend this, but when you tell it to the white man he shuts his mouth because he knows that this is true.

Then those who have studied a little deeper will say, "Before

God called it Christianity it was called Judaism" – isn't this what they say? Named after a man called Judah. Now this doesn't follow logically.

If Christianity was named after Christ was born, and before Christ was born the religion was called Judaism, then that means that it got its name from a son of Jacob whose name was Judah. But history tells us that Jacob was bending down [in prayer] before Judah was born, which shows us that Jacob's religion couldn't have been Judaism, and Isaac was Jacob's brother and he was bending down [in prayer] also before Jacob, his son was born. Isaac was Judah's grandfather and Abraham was Judah's great-grandfather, meaning that Abraham was on the scene long before Judah, and you couldn't call Abraham's religion Judaism because there was no such thing as Judaism in Abraham's day.

There was no such thing as Judaism in Isaac's day or in Jacob's day. Do you understand? So was God's religion before they called it Judaism? This is something that the white man has never taught you and me. The white man is afraid to let you and I know what God's religion was called in Abraham's day because Abraham is supposed to have been the father of all of them. He is supposed to have been one of God's first servants. One of the first to submit to God is supposed to have been Abraham. Now if you can see and understand this, then find out what Abraham's religion really was.

The Honorable Elijah Muhammad teaches us that Abraham's religion was the religion of Islam. Islam only means complete submission to God, complete obedience to God. Abraham obeyed God. Abraham obeyed God so much that when God told him to take his son and sacrifice him by sticking a dagger in his heart, isn't that what He said? Because Abraham took his only son up on a mountain and was going to sacrifice him to God, which shows Abraham completely believed in Islam.

What does Islam mean? Obey God. There is only one God and His name is Allah. Submit to God. So that this name [Malcom writes

"Islam" on the black board], if you notice, has no connection, no association, with the death of a man. This is not a man's name, this doesn't come from a man. Buddhism is named after a man called Buddha; Confucianism is named after a man called Confucius, right or wrong? Likewise with Judaism and Christianity. But Islam is not connected with any ["Human Beings"] name.

Islam is an act which means which means submit completely to God, or obey God. And when you say your religion is Islam that means you're a Muslim. So to clarify this what must you do? You must have a knowledge of history. If you don't have a knowledge of history you'll run around calling yourself a Christian when you're serving God, or you'll run around saying your religion is Judaism and you'll swear you're serving God. If your religion is Christianity you're following Christ, if your religion is Judaism you're following Judah, and if you're religion is Buddhism you're following Buddha, do you understand? And they are all dead, and if you follow them you'll die too. This is where it all leads you. Wherever your leaders go, that's what happens to you. Now we who follow the Honorable Elijah Muhammad, but we believe in the religion of Islam, we don't believe in Muhammad.

He teaches us the religion of Islam. Do you understand the difference? These people who follow Christ [pointing to the cross painted on the blackboard], they believe in Christ; many of them believe Christ is God-Oh yes, they do; that he was born of the Blessed Virgin, didn't have a father, was just a spirit, and then came into the world and was crucified, rose from the dead, and went up into space. They believe that, but they believe it because they don't know history. But if you notice, the Euro-Jew whites have a better knowledge of true history than the Christians do, do they not? The Christians' history only goes back two thousand years; the history of the Jews [the original black Hebrew Jew then much later-on in history was the white man looking converted Euro-Jew], goes back beyond four thousand years. Can you see this? However, the

Muslim history goes back...there is no time limit to the Muslim history.

If you notice, the Christian can only go back to what they call the Greek Empire. That's what they call the Occidental, the beginning of the Occident, is the Greek Empire, the Roman Empire, and so forth. The Jews have a knowledge that goes back to black man's Egypt and Babylon. You notice how one goes back...it has no limit. There are no chains on how far you can go back when you are a Muslim. The Christians and the Euro-Jews go back to whom? To Adam, and they stop right there. And they say beyond him nothing was happening. The greater their knowledge of history is, this has an influence on the type of religion that they accept. Do you understand?

All praise is due to Allah. Another example: what makes the royal family of Europe, or any country, differ from the peasant? Royalty knows its ancestry, and royalty knows its history, this is what makes them royal. You can't have a king who can't trace his family tree history back through his forefathers. The only way you can be a king is to be born a king. If you take away his history [like whites did the Negro slave], and he doesn't know who his forefathers were, what does he become? A peasant, a common ordinary man. The same is with the Jews and Christians. It's because the Jews [original or Euro], have the longest record of history that they call themselves the "Chosen People" which is the original, that that Euro wanna be lie, claiming to be God's "Chosen People." [Were **black people;** God's "Chosen People"].

The Christians can't call themselves the Chosen People because their history is not long enough. They can't go back to the time when the choice was being made. The Hebrews, the so-called Euro Jews, can go back so far they can lay claim to that which, is actually not theirs. But the reason they can falsely claim it is that nobody else they are dealing with can go back far enough to disprove them [is where they hide truth that's evil, is their wrong]. Except the

Muslims. Do you understand? So the Honorable Elijah Muhammad's mission is to teach the so-called Negroes (Today's **Nubian Americans**), a knowledge of history, the history of ourselves, our own kind, showing us how we fit into prophecy, "Biblical Prophecy."

When you go to one of the churches you will notice that it is named after some word in their Bible: Big Rock Baptist Church, or Drinking at the Well Baptist Church, Friendship Baptist Church, Union Baptist, Israel Baptist, Jacob's ladder Baptist, and different first names of Churches of God in Christ etc. They find some kind of old perhaps, funny word in their Bible to name their whole religion after. Their whole doctrine is based on a verse in the Bible: "He rose."

The Honorable Elijah Muhammad bases what he teaches not on verse but on the entire book. And from beginning to end, he says he can open up the Book and prove that the Bible agrees with him, and then can use the Bible to prove that [some of] what they are teaching in the church is wrong. You know that's saying something.

For instance, he says that in Genesis, the fifteenth chapter and thirteenth verse, just to give you an example: "And He said unto Abram, know of a surety that thy seed shall be a stranger in a land that is not theirs, and shall serve them; and they shall afflict them four hundred years; and also that nation, whom they shall serve, will I judge: and afterward shall they come out with great substance. [substance 4 : material possessions : PROPERTY, WEALTH]. Now the Honorable Elijah Muhammad says that explains his teachings right there because he teaches that the so-called Negro [African American correct identity that's Nubian American], is the one that the Bible is talking about. Who have spent 400 years and are strangers in a land that is not theirs? And you can't deny that we are strangers here. I don't think any of you will deny that we are not in a country where we are made to feel at home. We'll put it that way.

There is hardly any Negro in his right mind who can say he

feels right at home in America. He has to admit that he is made to feel like a stranger. Right or wrong? Well this is what God said to Abraham would happen in this day and time. Remember, Abraham's religion was Islam. Abraham wasn't a Jew, Abraham wasn't a Christian, Abraham wasn't a Buddhist, Abraham was a Muslim, which means he obeyed God. God told him, yes. He said, your people are going into bondage, they're going to become slaves, they're going to be afflicted, they'll be strangers in a land far from home for 400 years.

The Honorable Elijah Muhammad says you and I are the seed of Abraham, we're the descendants of Abraham. Now the preacher in the church, he tells you that The Jews (white looking Euro-Jews) are of the seed of Abraham. Now, one of them is right and one of them is very wrong: either Mr. Muhammad is right and the preacher is wrong, or the preacher is right and Mr. Muhammad is very wrong. This is what we are putting on the line and table today.

Who is the seed of Abraham? Is it this blue-eyed, blond-haired, pale-skin Jew? Or is it the so-called Negro, [then called African American, but correct identity is Nubian American] – you? [Since a Jew can be born in Africa, and called an African but was his heritage-culture born of Africa?] So who is it? And what makes it so pitiful, many of our people would rather believe that the Jews are God's Chosen People. They would rather believe that the Jew is better than anybody else. This is a Negro. Nobody else would put everybody else above him but the [ill-informed] Negro.

I mean the American Negro. Remember, God said that the people would be strangers. The Jews aren't strangers. The Jews know their history, the Jews know their culture, the Jews know their language; they know everything there is to know about themselves. They know how to rob you, they know how to be your landlord, they know how to be your grocer, they know how to be your lawyer, they know how to join the NAACP and become the president, right or wrong? They know how to control everything you've got. You can't say their lost. But the poor so-called Negro, he doesn't control the NAACP, he can't control the Urban League, he can't control his own schools, he can't control his own businesses in his own community. He can't even control his own mind. He's lost and lost control of himself and gone astray.

But he fits the picture here that the Bible says concerning our people in the last day: "Know of a surety that that thy seed shall be a stranger in a land that is not theirs, and shall serve them." And you have served the white man; he hasn't served you and me. Why, the Jew hasn't served anybody here. You are the one that's serving: "And they shall afflict them 400 years; and also that nation, whom they shall serve, will I judge: and afterwards shall they come out with great substance." Oft times when you say this to the so-called Negroes they'll come up and tell you that this is the Jew. But if you'll notice, when Jesus was talking to the Jews, way back here in John, he told them that they shall know the truth and it will make them free. The Jews popped up and said: "How are you going to say that we shall be made free? We have never been in bondage to anyone." Isn't that what the Jews told Jesus? Now look at it. If the Jews said to Jesus, 2,000 years after Moses supposedly led the Hebrews out of bondage, that they had never been in bondage, know you know the Jews had Moses' history, they knew who Moses was, how could they stand up and tell Jesus they had never been in bondage? Not these things that you call Jew.

They weren't in Egypt, they weren't the people that Moses led out of Egypt, and the Jews know this. But the Bible is written in such a tricky way, when you read it you think that Moses led the Jews out of bondage. But if you get a Jew in a good solid conversation today and you know how to talk to him, he'll have to admit this, that it wasn't out of bondage that Moses brought them, it was out of somewhere else, and where Moses really brought them is their secret, but, thanks to Almighty God, the Honorable Elijah Muhammad knows their secret, and told it to us and we're going to tell it to you, [was the dark caves of Europe].

If the Holy Bible said that God is going to judge that nation, the nation that enslaved His Chosen People, how would he keep from destroying His own people? The same Bible is a book of history and the 18th chapter of the book of Deuteronomy, in the 18th verse, God told Moses: "I will raise them up a prophet" talking about you and me, I'll raise them up a prophet just like thee – a prophet like Moses whose mission it would be to do for you and me the same thing that Moses did back then. It would be a prophet like Moses. In fact, when you get down to Malachi, He lets it be known that just before He comes to Judge that nation, the name of the prophet or messenger whom He would send among the people would be Elijah.

It says: Before the coming of that great and dreadful day I shall send you Elijah and Elijah's job will be to turn the hearts of the children to the fathers and the hearts of the fathers to the children. What does this mean, turn the hearts of the children to the fathers? The so-called Negro are childlike people, you're like children. No matter how old you get, or how bold you get, or how wise you get, or how rich you get, or how educated you might get, the white man still [in mockery] calls you what? "A Boy!" Why, are you still a child in the Jews and white man's eyesight!

And you are a child anytime you let another man set up a factory for you and you can't for yourself, you're a child; anytime another man has to open up businesses for you and you don't know how to open up businesses for yourself and your people, you're a child; anytime another man sets up schools and you don't know how to set up your own schools, you're a child. Because a child is someone who sits around and waits for his father to do for him, what he should be doing for himself…I hate to say it but it's the truth, all you and I seems to have done is build churches and let the white man build factories. ["Slavery," took its toll on the black man. Slavery from the white man tried to strip the black man from of all his knowledge of self, in America, separated by two oceans for secrecy and no interferences, on both sides of her. He created the child like responds from the black man, to advance over the white man's obstacles and road-blocks put in front of you and I. However, nothing remains the same it is said, including the black man, to rise above evil Satan, and his devils; the Euro-Jew and the white man in America, is the Biblical prophecy].

But it seems, still you and I build churches and let the white man build schools. You and I build churches and let the white man build up everything for himself. Then after you build the church you have to go and beg the white man for a job, and beg the white man for some education. Am I right or wrong? Do you see what I mean? It' too bad, [pitiable], but it's true. And it's also history. So it shows that these childlike people, people who would be children, following after the [devious] white man. It says in the last days that God will raise up Elijah, and Elijah's job will be to turn the hearts of these children back toward their fathers. Elijah will come [as Biblically prophesized] and change our minds; he'll teach us something that will change and turn us completely around. When Elijah finds us [it's strange that], **"we'll be easy to lead in the wrong direction but hard to lead in the right direction."** But when Elijah gets through teaching the "Lost Sheep," or the "Lost People" of God, he'll turn them around to the truth, he'll change their minds, he'll put a board in their back, making them throw their shoulders back, and stand upright, tall like men for the first time. It says he'll turn the hearts of these children toward their fathers and the hearts of the fathers toward the children.

This is something that the Honorable Elijah Muhammad is doing here in America today. Because you and I haven't thought in terms of our forefathers. We haven't thought of our fathers. Our fathers, brothers, are back home, our **"homeland."** [And not the white man trying to act like some sort of "God"-father, but is a hood-wink shepherd of deception, to the lost black sheep]. Our fathers are in the **"East"**... You never hear of black people in this country talking or speaking or thinking in terms of **connecting** themselves with their own kind back home. [Instead], they are trying to make contact with the white man, trying to connect, trying to make a connection with a kidnapper who brought them here, trying to make a connection with actually, the very man who enslaved them. Now you know that's a shame, it's painfully pitiful, but it's **true**.

The Honorable Elijah Muhammad says that when Elijah comes, the Book says when Elijah comes, what Elijah will do is to teach these people the truth. And the truth that Elijah will teach the people would be so strong it will make all that other stuff that the preachers are talking about sound like a fairy tale story. Elijah will open the people's eyes up so wide that from then on a preacher won't be able to talk to them and this is really true. Do you know, people have come to Muhammad's Mosque and no matter whether they believe in what Mr. Muhammad was saying or not they never could go back and sit in Church. This is true. What the Honorable Elijah Muhammad does is to turn on the light, and when he turns on the light it enables us to see and think for ourselves. He shows us that what the white man has taught us concerning history has actually been a distortion. He's never given you and me true facts about history, neither about himself nor about our people.

You know I read a book one day called the Four Cities of Troy. You can go to the library, some libraries, and check it out. What was this based on? To show you what a liar the white man is. When I say liar: you have white people who are scientists and keep truth in their own circles, and they never let you or the masses anything about the truth kept in the circle... So in this particular book it pointed out that some archaeologists were delving in the ruins of the ancient city of Troy, and in the practice of digging to the city of Troy they dug deeper than they intended to, ran into the ruins of another city that had been there so much longer than the city of

Troy that it had gone down beneath the sands of time, and they had built this city of Troy on top of it…they learned that there were ruins of a city more ancient than that. So they started frantically digging onto that one and dug some more until they found another one and before they got through digging they had dug down and they had discovered that civilizations in that area had been there so far back into history that at different times in history some of the cities had been destroyed, had become completely covered up with sand and dirt, until another people came along and didn't even know it was there and built another civilization on top of it.

This happened four different times, to give you some idea of what the white man knows concerning the length of time man has been on this earth, and still that white man would jump up in your face and try to make you believe that the first man was made 6,000 years ago named Adam. And a lot of [unknowing] Negroes will want to know what you are talking about, Adam, that's what God called him. God took some dirt and breathed on it and told Adam, "Come forth," and there he was. Now you know very well that's a shame [a painful sense of having done something wrong, improper, or immodest: DISGRACE…

It' alright to believe when you were a little baby that God made a little doll out of sand and mud and breathed on it and that was the first man. But here it is 1962 with all this information floating around in everybody's ears, you can get it free. Why, you should open up you minds and your heads and your hearts and realize that you have been led by a lie.

Today it's time to listen to nothing but naked, undiluted truth. And when you know the truth, as [Nubian] Jesus said: "The truth will set you free." Abraham Lincoln won't make you free. Truth will make you free. When you know the truth, you're free. Also you have your archaeologists, anthropologists and other forms of historians who agree that they don't know how long man has been on earth, but they do know that man has been on earth longer than

6,000 years. They know that man was not made just 6,000 years ago [except for a certain kind of man]. They know this now but a long time ago they didn't know it.

There was a time when they believed that a man had fewer ribs than a woman. You can believe that because **"they"** said that God made Eve from one of Adam's ribs, so Adam had a rib missing. And they actually ran around here believing for many years that man had one less rib, and they were shook up began to wonder then what happened [in writing the KJV – King James Version] in the Bible?

[This book will remind the world, will give the world a reality-check justifiably, just who we Nubians really are in history when there was no white people in existence, in **prehistory.** If you know your history then you and I know that white Christian Nationalist Patriots means racism against the black man for a white man only America. The bottom line of racism trying to destroy **"democracy"** in America, is Trump in office, a wealthy low-life liar and his constituency who are worried about the "blackening and browning of America," is the fear of them losing their power, a punk bullying, wanting to control everything. But we Nubian Americans as activists, must rise up, obeying God, we'll overcome receiving great substance! Because, how can you, or anyone else take joy out of innocent others pain and racist miseries, from a want to be dictator you, Trump? Who needs to be **kicked** in his, stupid, no empathy, **rear-end**, for real! A convicted felon of 34 counts running the white-house, must end now with removal, who would rather see this great country burn; then give-in to qualified **representatives,** people of color, running it; who ignorant white-supremacist wrongly surmise, means owning America.]

How long has man been here? In the Bible in the chapter of Genesis and the twenty-six verse, after God had made everything else it says: And God said, let us make man." Let me write what God said here on the board…look what God said brothers. I don't think you ever looked at this. It says: "And God said, let us make man." The key word here is what? Yes, what does "us" mean? More than one. Who was God talking to? If God was all by Himself, no one was their but Him, who was He talking to when He said, let us make man?" Who was there with God who was about to help Him make this man?

When God was getting ready to make the sun He didn't say, "Let us make some sun!" He said, "Let there be light." And here is the sun, a ball of fire 2,678,785 miles in circumference, 853,000 miles in diameter, 17,072 degrees hot – that's a whole lot of heat. And God said, "Let there be," and that big ball of fire popped up there in the universe. He didn't ask for no help: "let there be this and let there be that." He had so much power that everything he wanted came into existence; as soon as He said "be," there it was. But when He got to man something happened, someone else was there, wasn't there? That's something to think about. We let you think about it for a minute.

The White man's world is a newer world than the Black man's world. If this man said that they were about to make man, and he said we would make him how – in – your image – this shows you that there's somebody there with Him. "Let us make man on our image, in our likeness. Let us make him look like us. He won't be the same as we are, he'll be in our image." That's God talking, right? He's talking to somebody. You know, I'm thankful to Allah for raising up the Honorable Elijah Muhammad and making us see things that we could never see before

The birth of the white race has always been a **"SECRET."** The Honorable Elijah Muhammad says that the white race is shrouded in the story of Adam. The story of Adam **hides** the birth of the white race, and because you and I have never been taught to look into a thing and analyze a thing we took the story of Adam exactly as it was. We thought that God made a man named Adam six thousand years ago. But today the Honorable Elijah Muhammad teaches us that man, Adam, was a white man; that before Adam was made the black man was already here. The white man will even tell you that, because he refers to Adam as the first one. He refers to the **Adamites** as those who came from that first one. He refers to the Adamites as those who were here before Adam. Right or wrong? Those people who were here before Adam. And he always refers to these people as **"aborigines,"** which means? **BLACK FOLK!!!!**

You'll never find a white aborigine. Aborigines are called natives, and they're always dark-skinned people. You and I are aborigines. But you don't like to be called an aborigine; you want to be an American. Aborigine actually means, "From the beginning." It's two Latin words, "ab" meaning "from;" "origin" meaning "the beginning;" and aborigine is only the term applied to those dark-skinned people who have been on this earth since the beginning of the universe. You know that's going way back. What do you mean, since the beginning of the universe?

Three-fourths of the Earth's surface is covered with water. So you say since it's the natural law for water to seek its own level why doesn't it overrun the land? The Honorable Elijah Muhammad says that as the Earth speeds around the sun turning on its axis 1,037 1/3 miles per hour it creates gravity and the strong attracting power of the sun pulls on the water of the Earth, drawing them up into the atmosphere in fine mist that the naked eye can hardly detect. The power of the moon is not as great as that of the sun, but since it can't pull the waters up like the does, it still has that magnetic pull and it causes the waves that you see out there on the ocean to churn... It never lets them level out. If they leveled out the water would overrun the land. The trap the white man put us in, thinking that the only one who can do anything is a Mystery God and what the Mystery God doesn't do the white man does.

When the moon was blasted away, [a theory I must admit I don't agree with of Islamic science] and we came along with the Earth, one tribe was in fact destroyed...the thirteenth tribe was destroyed and then all of the time down through the wheel of time since then there were twelve tribes until six thousand years ago. And six thousand years ago, a scientist named **Yakub** created another tribe on this Earth. ...It was made different from all of the twelve tribes, [The 12 tribes of original Israel], that were here when it arrived. A new tribe, a weak tribe, a devilish tribe, a diabolical tribe, a tribe that is devilish by nature. So that before they got on the scene, The Honorable Elijah Muhammad says that when we came with the Earth, the oldest city on Earth is the Holy City, Mecca, in Arabia. Mecca is the oldest city on Earth.

[In all respect, however we here differ with it being in the Sudan, Africa's **Nubian** cities is believed one of them the oldest city on Earth]. Mecca is the city that is forbidden. NO one can go there but the black man. No one can go there but the Muslims. No one can go there but the believer. No one can go there but the righteous. And at Mecca are kept the records of history that go back to the beginning of time. [Today, it is with white believers in prayer also.]

He says that fifty thousand years ago another scientist named **Shabazz** became angry with the scientists of his day. He wanted to bring about a tougher people. He wanted the people to undergo a form of life that would make them tough and hard, and the other scientists wouldn't agree with him. So, this scientist named Shabazz took his family and wandered down into the jungles of Africa. Prior to that time no one lived in the jungles of Africa. Our people were soft; they were black, but they were soft and delicate, fine. They had straight hair. Right here on this Earth you find some of them look like that today.

They are black as night, but their hair is as silk, and originally all our people had that kind of hair. But the scientist took his family down into the jungles of Africa. [It is a fact that doing the beginning, Nubian/Ethiopian, many Ethiopian blacks had silky straight hair and believed many migrated, making the India population.] And living in the open, living a jungle life, eating all kinds of food had an effect on the appearance of our people. Actually, living in the rough climate, our hair became stiff, like it is now. The Honorable Elijah Muhammad says that the only hair that the black man has today that looks now like it looked prior to fifty thousand years ago is your and my eyebrows. Right here you notice, all Negroes has straight – I don't care how nappy their hair is – they have straight eyebrows. When you see a nappy-hair-eyebrow Negro [chuckle] you got somebody. But all of this took place back in history, and everything the Honorable Elijah Muhammad teaches is based on history. Now then, where does this white man come in?

So when he says the wise blackman of the East writes history a year of every mile, he writes history to last 25,000 years – not in the past, but in the future. He says that on this Earth there are wise black men who can tune in and tell what's going to happen in the future just as clear – they can see ahead just as clear – as they can see the past. And every 25,000 years he says that civilization reaches its peak or reaches its perfection. At this time the wise black man sits down and write history to last for 25,000 years. After this history expires they put it in a vault at the Holy City, Mecca, and write a new history.

And they discovered that in the year 8,400 [BC] to come, it would register that among five billion black people, seventy percent would be satisfied, and thirty percent would be dissatisfied. And out of that thirty percent would be born a wise black scientist named Yakub, and Yakub would teach among these thirty percent dissatisfied form whom he would come, and create a new race, start a new world, and a new civilization that would rule this Earth for six thousand years to come. So they brought these findings back to the King and they were put in a book. And by the way, that which is written to last 25,000 years is called the **Holy Koran.**

The Honorable Elijah Muhammad said that this was put into the history and then when the year 8400 BC came, Yakub was born. When Yakub reached the age of six years he was playing in the sand one day with two pieces of metal, two pieces of steel, at which time he discovered what is known as the law of magnetism: that unalike attracts and like repeals. Two objects that are alike repeal each other like two women, like two men repel each other, but man and woman attract each other. Unalike attracts and like repels. Yakub discovered this. So Yakub knew that all he had to do was make a man unalike any other man on Earth and because he would be different he would attract all other people. Then he could teach this man a science called tricknology, which is a science of tricks and lies, and this weak man would be able to use that science to trick and rob and rule the world.

So Yakub turned to his and said, "When I grow up I'm going to make a man who will rule you." And Yakub's uncle said, "What can you make other than that which will cause bloodshed and wickedness in the land?" And Yakub pointed to his head and said, "I know that which you know not." Yakub was born with a determined idea to make a man because it had been predicted 8400 years prior to his birth that he would be born to do his work. So he was born with this idea in him, and when his uncle realized that this was about whom it had been prophesied his uncle submitted. The Honorable Elijah Muhammad said that Yakub went to school in the East; he studied the astronomical sciences, mathematical sciences, and the germination of man.

He discovered that in the black man there are two germs. In the black man there's a brown man. In the black man, or the black germ, which is a strong germ, there's a weak germ, a brown germ. Yakub was the first one to discover this and Yakub knew that by separating that brown one from the black one, and then grafting the brown one from the black one so that it became lighter and lighter, it would eventually reach its lightest stage which is known as white. And when it got to that stage it would be weak it would be susceptible to wickedness. [The "reason" being susceptible to **wickedness** by nature who can shoot to kill innocent Nubian Americans ex-slaves – the author]. And then Yakub could take that weak man that he made and teach him how to lie and rob and cheat and thereby become the ruler of all the rest of the world.

So, The Honorable Elijah Muhammad teaches us that Yakub began to preach at the age of sixteen. He began to preach all over Arabia in the East. He preached among the thirty percent who were dissatisfied and got many of them to follow him. As they began to listen to Yakub's teachings and believed them, his teachings spread, his followers grew, and it created confusion in the land. The Honorable Elijah Muhammad says that so much confusion came into existence over there they threw Yakub's followers in **"jail,"** and as fast as they would throw them in jail they taught more people. So the teachings spread in jail. Finally, Yakub was put in jail, under an alias. And one day, The honorable Elijah Muhammad says, the thing began to get out of hand and the authorities went to the King and told him that they couldn't control these people, but that they had the leader of the people in jail right now, and the King said, "Take me to him."

And when the King went to the jail where Yakub was, he greeted Yakub "As-Salaam-Alaikum, Mr. Yakub" – I know you're Mr. Yakub – and Yakub said, "Wa-Alaikum-Salaam" – I am Yakub! And the King said, "Look, I come to make an agreement with you. I know that you are the one that it is written or predicted would be on the scene in this day and would create a new race, and there is nothing I can do to stop you. But in order for us to have peace we want to make an agreement with you. In order to stop the confusion and for there to be some peace in the land, we want you to take all who will follow you and exile yourselves out on an island in the Aegean Sea."

Yakub told them, "I'll go. But you've got to give me everything that I will need to bring into existence a new civilization. You've got to give me everything I'll need. You've got to supply me with everything I'll need for the next twenty-years." And The Honorable Elijah Muhammad says that the King agreed with Yakub, the government of that day agreed to supply Yakub and his followers with everything they needed for twenty years. And he says he gets this from the Bible where it says Jacob wrestled with the angel. Jacob was Yakub, and the angel that Jacob wrestled with wasn't God, it was the government of that day. "Angel only means "a power," or somebody with power.

When a man has his wings clipped, you say he has lost his power, wrestled with an angel, "angel" is only used as a symbol to hide the one he was really wrestling with. Jacob was wrestling with the government of that day gave him everything he needed to last him and his followers for twenty years...

The honorable Elijah Muhammad teaches us that Yakub agreed, the government agreed, Yakub took all of his followers down to the sea. Yakub took 59,999 of his followers down to the seaside, with himself making 60,000. He piled them on boats and took them out to an Island in the Aegean Sea called Pelan. In the Bible it's called **"Patmos."** When you read in the book of Revelation where John, on the Island of Patmos, heard the word of the Lord that is Yakub. What was John doing on the Island of Patmos? John was out there getting ready to make a new race, he said, for the word of the Lord. What was the word of the Lord? The word was that in the year 8400 a new man would be made; a new race would be made. And when Yakub and his followers got out there his followers realized that Yakub was wiser than any man of his day, and they recognized him as a god; he was a god to them.

So when you get to the place in the Bible where it says, "And God said, Let us make man," that was **"Yakub"** too, not the Supreme Being. It wasn't the Supreme Being who made the sun who said, **"Let us make man."** When the Supreme Being made the sun he said, let there be light." He said He was supreme. He was independent, and He needed no help, no associates. But when it came to making a man, that god said, "Let us make man." He didn't speak with independence, because there were two different gods. God the Supreme Being made the light. His word is "be;" that's how He made things. But Yakub, who was lesser god, said to 59,000 of his followers, "Let us make man, and let us make a man in or image, in our likeness. We are going to make a white man."

It was Yakub talking: "Make him in our image and in our likeness and give him dominion over the fowl of the air and the fish of the sea and the creatures of the land. And we'll call him Adam." It's only a name for the white man. The white man has taken mastery over the air, his airplanes rule the sky, his submarines and ships rule the sea, and his armies rule the land. This was the man that was made six thousand years ago and the purpose for making him was so he could rule the world for six thousand years. That's the white man.

The Honorable Elijah Muhammad says that the first thing Yakub did was to get his ministers, doctors, nurses, and cremators together. He gave them the laws because he had to set up a birth control law. He told the doctors whenever two black ones come to him to get married to stick a needle in their veins, take some blood, and go back and tell them that their blood doesn't match so they can't marry. He also said when a black one and a brown one come, let them get married, or if two brown ones come let them get married. Then he told the nurse nine months after their married, when you're ready to deliver their child, if it's a black child, put a needle in its brain and feed it to a wild animal or give it to the cremator. Let it be destroyed. But if it's a brown child, take that child to the mother and tell her that this is going to be a great man when he grows up because he's lighter than that the others.

Tell her that the child you destroyed was an angel baby and it went up to heaven to prepare a place for her when she dies. Same old lie they tell you today – when a little baby dies he goes to the same place a mangoes when he dies – right down into the ground. Is that right or wrong? So the honorable Elijah Muhammad has taught us that Yakub right there set up birth control law. Within two hundred years they had killed off all black babies on the Island. Everything black had been destroyed. And then Yakub only lived 150 years. But he left laws and rules and regulations behind, for his follower to go by. And after they had destroyed all the black ones on the island of Pelan, they began to work on the brown germ. They saved the yellow and destroyed the brown, because you see in the black there's brown and in the brown there's yellow.

Can you see how it goes? The darker one all ways has a lighter one in it. So in the black man there's a brown man, in the brown man there's a yellow man, in the yellow man there's what? A white man. Oh yes. Getting weaker all the time. So it took two hundred years to destroy the black. And then they worked on the brown for two hundred years. And in two hundred years all the brown was destroyed and all they had on the island of Pelan was a yellow or **Mulatto**-looking civilization. And then they went to work on it and began to destroy it. So that after six hundred years of destruction on the island of Pelan, they had grafted away the black, grafted away the brown, grafted away the yellow, so that all they had left was a pale-skinned, blue-eyed, blonde-haired thing that you call a man. But actually, the **Bible** calls him the **"Devil."**

That's the devil that the Bible is talking about, old **Lucifer, Satan,** or the **serpent.** Because the lighter they got, the weaker they got. As they began to get lighter and lighter, they grew weaker, and weaker. Their blood became weaker, their bones became weaker, their minds became weaker, and their morals became weaker. They became a wicked race; by **"nature"** wicked. Why by nature?

The Book says concerning the devil: "He was conceived in inequity (unjustness) and born in sin. "What does this mean? At the outset the nurses had to kill the little black babies, but after a while it got so that the mother, having been brainwashed, hated that black one so much she killed it herself. Killed it herself and saved the light one, and right on down for six hundred years. In order for the white one to come into existence, the darker one was always murdered, murdered, MURDERED! This went right into the nature [trait – an inherited characteristic] of the child that was being born. The mother wanted a light baby when the child was being conceived. This went right into the baby.

So that at the end of the six hundred years, after planting the seed of inequity right into the brain, right into the mind, right into the heart, right into the nature of these people, by the time by the time they got the white man, they had someone who by nature hated everything that was darker than he was. They had to murder off the black, brown, and yellow in order to get to white. And right to this very day the white man by nature wants to murder off the black, brown, and yellow. You don't have to teach him to kill the black man. He does it for sport. ["I can't breathe," said Floyd, "your knee on my neck killing me, Momma, Momma...!" The author here.] Do you understand that?

So in six hundred years now they got a devil on the scene, a blue-eyed devil, blond haired. Oh yes, they were out there on the island of Pelan. Yakub was dead. Yakub was their **father,** but he never saw them. Yakub was their **god.** When the Bible says no man has seen God, that's what it means. No white man has ever seen their god. Not one of them saw Yakub because Yakub only lived to be a 150 years old ... So after they were out there six hundred years, after they were made and grafted and Yakub was dead, then they packed up their bags and made it back to **civilization.** Yakub had left them some laws to go by.

He left them a **science** called "Tricknology:" how to **"divide and conquer."** Yakub told these people in his book: all you got to do to take over the world is to **lie.** Go back among the people... You see, he's an *underdog. He's a minority. This is the trick that the white man was born to execute among dark mankind here on this Earth. Yakub said, "When you go back among them, lie about them to each other, and when they start fighting, ask them to let you be the **mediator.** And soon as you become the mediator then you're the boss." "Let us make man," all began with Yakub's, **"Graphtation."** The white man's crowning glory was with the Native American, the Indians.

The white man has done this trick everywhere. Here in America to the Indians. He sent one priest to the Indians in New York and another priest to the Indians in Pennsylvania and both of them would tell lies to both Indians, and the Indians who had never been at war with each other would start beating the tom-toms, the war drums, and then they got ready to fight the priest would run in and say, "Let me be the mediator." So he told the New York Indians, you move out to Minnesota; and the Pennsylvania Indians, you move out to Oklahoma. That would leave the whole states of New York and Pennsylvania for the white man. You see how he does it? He's all over the world. He's a mediator. He's an **instigator** and mediator. He instigates division dissension and soon as they start fighting one another he says, "OK, I'll settle it." If you don't think so look all over the world right now. Every place on this earth you have a division: South Korea – North Korea, South Vietnam – North Vietnam. [Much less North America – South America.] Right or wrong?

He is the one that makes this decision, he doesn't let anybody get together, but when it comes to his kind he's united. United States means all white people united. United States of Europe, or European Common Market – they want to get together. But when you start talking about a United States of Asia, or a **"United States of Africa,"** why he says, "Oh **NO,** too many different languages [chuckle]. You all don't have anything in common." You see how he does it? He always discourages unity among others, but he encourages unity among his own kind. "United We Stand," that doesn't mean you. That means the white man. The white man is [as being] the one who stand united.

So the Honorable Elijah Muhammad says that these devils went back into **Arabia.** When they got there they started telling **lies,** started confusion and in six months' time they had turned "heaven into **hell.** Oh yeh, they had so much fighting going on among our people, brother, it became hell… And when these devils came back into our mist they turned our **"paradise"** into hell. So it was taken to the King and the King looked into the book and said, "Why, these are Yakub's people." He said, "They were made to do what they're doing and the

67

only way to have peace is to get rid of them. So the King gave the order for all of the devils to be rounded up.

He gave orders for them to be rounded up there in the East, and they were rounded and taken down to the edge of the Arabian **Desert.** They were stripped naked, stripped of everything except their language. The Honorable Elijah Muhammad says that we put lambskin aprons around their waists to hide their nakedness. We put them in chains and marched them across the hot sands of the Arabian Desert. This is what the black man did to the white man, brothers [who can't refute the truth that was written]. This is what the gods did to the devils. Actually, if you think I don't know what I'm talking about, those of you who are **Masons,** you go through this and don't understand it.

When you go in, they put a lambskin apron around your waist. They put you in what's called the "cable tow." Right or wrong? And then they make you jump up and down on an electric mat. Make you take off your shoes and put the juice in the mat and make you jump up and down. Why? What are they getting at? That's all a sign of what happened to the white man six thousand years ago. It just doesn't have anything to do with you, but you're supposed to be walking on hot sands when you jump up and down. Right or wrong? You've been in some of that stuff. They tell you that's crossing the hot sand. And if you walk up to a Negro Mason and ask him, "When you crossed the hot sand were you walking or riding?" He'll say, "I was walking."

He's a fool. Because he was riding. He was riding horseback. He was riding on a camel. It was the white man that was in chains. It was the white man that had the apron around him. It was the white man that was walking the white sand. We walked them at high noon. We wouldn't even let them walk at night. We stopped at night. And you know how hot the sun and the sands are in Arabia.

We expected the white man to die when we were running him out of the East... He lived. A lot of them died on the desert. And if I might come back – all of this is tied up in the **Masonic** ritual. When a man gets initiated into the higher order goes through this. They put on the chains, they put on the aprons, and they darken him up and pretend to be driving him across. Then when he gets up to the top order in those degrees, they tell him what it means. The white man, they tell the white man what it means; a white **Shriner,** a white Mason, what it means. A Negro never learns what it means. But actually points back towards the time when the white man, who is the **devil** [Christ even called him], or Adam, as they say, was cast out the **Garden.** When the Bible says Adam sinned and was cast out of the garden, this is what is meant.

And an angel was put at the East gate to keep him from coming back in. When the white man was run out of the East by the Muslims six thousand years ago into the caves of Europe, the people called **Turks** were put there at the straits of the Dardanelles, with swords, and any old devil that they caught trying to come back across the water – WHOP! – Off went his head. The Book tells you that the angel had a flaming sword, and any time any of them tried to come back across they were put to death. [Now you know question answered why China built the **"Great Wall of China!"** Remember: the above is from 33 and 1/3 to 360 the highest degrees of knowledge and wisdom in the Masonic Order; then there's the Eastern Star of the Negro women.]

The Honorable Elijah Muhammad says that the white man went down into the caves of Europe and he lived there for two thousand years… Within one thousand years after he had gotten there [it is said] he was on all fours, couldn't stand upright. [Perhaps from the desert crossing.] Within one thousand years after he had gotten there he was on all fours, couldn't stand up right… But those who have some education, they straighten up a little bit because they're taught how to straighten up… You have to put a white man on the **"square."** [The square of truth.] But a black man can be the most dumb, illiterate thing you can find anywhere, and he still walks like a million dollars because by nature he's upright, by nature he stands up... You have to put a white man on the square. But the black man is born on the square.

Can we prove it? Yes. You notice in the East, dark people carry things on their heads, don't they? Just throw it up there and walk with it, showing you, they have perfect **"poise,"** perfect balance. It just natural to them. You and I lost our poise. We, you, can't even wear a hat on your head, hardly, today [chuckle]. [But we still got our great "dignity & pride."]

The honorable Elijah Muhammad says that within one thousand years after the white people were up in the caves ...they were living in the outdoors where it's cold, just as cold over there as it is outside right now. They didn't have clothes. So by being out there in the cold their hair got longer and longer. Hair grew all over their bodies. [Many] were on all fours ... Oh yes brother, up in the caves of Europe...

The only thing that made friends with the white man was the dog. He'd sit outside of the cave...and if any beast came up and tried to get in the cave at his family, he'd throw rocks at it, or he'd have a club that he'd swing down and try to drive it away with it. But the dog stayed in the cave with his family. It was then that the dog and the white man was **amalgamated** (to unite, or merge into one body). The white woman went with the dog while they were living in the caves of Europe. And right to this very day the white woman will tell you there is nothing she loves better than a dog.

They tell you that a dog is a man's best friend. They lived in that cave with those dogs and right now they got that dog smell. They got that dog...they are dog lovers. A dog can get in a white man's house and eat at his table, lick out of his plate. They'll kiss the dog right on the nose and think nothing of it. You're not a dog kisser. You don't see black people kissing or rubbing noses with dogs. But little white children will hug dogs and kiss dogs and eat with dogs. Am I right or wrong? You – all have been inside their kitchens cooking their food, and making their beds, you know how they live.

The dog will live right in the white man's house, better than you can; you try and break your way in there and they'll put a rope around your neck [chuckle], but the dog has got free run of the whole house. He's the white man's best friend.

The Honorable Elijah Muhammad says that they lived up there for two thousand years, and at the end of two thousand years the scientists in the East, realizing that it was originally predestined that the white race would rule for six thousand years, and that they already lost two thousand years in the caves of Europe, sent a prophet up there, from **Mecca,** to teach the white race, the race of devils, how to become civilized again, and become up right, and come back and **rule** the way they had originally been meant to. The name of that prophet was [black man] **Moses.**

Moses never went down into Egypt. Moses went into the caves of **Europe** and civilized the white man. It was Moses who raised the devil from a dead level to a perpendicular [up right] and placed him on the square. Moses **taught** the white man how to cook his food. Moses taught the white man how to build a house for himself. He taught the white man also some of the tricknology that Yakub had originally meant for him, and it was Moses who put the white man back on the road toward **"civilization."** He told him that he was supposed to rule for six thousand years, but that much of the time had already been lost, and at the end of time one would come who would destroy the whole white race. Moses taught them this.

And this is why when the Jews, two thousand years later was looking for the Messiah, they thought that Jesus was the Messiah and they him to death because they knew when the Messiah came he was going to destroy that whole race of devils. The Jews [Euro] knew this, so they put him to death thinking that they could stop him from destroying them. But actually, they made a mistake because Jesus two thousand years ago wasn't the Messiah. Their time wasn't up two thousand years ago. Their time would not be up until two thousand years later, the day and time that we're living in right now.

So brothers and sisters, my time has expired. I just wanted to point out that the white man, a race of devils was made six thousand years ago. This doesn't mean to tell you that this implies **"any kind of hate."** They're just a race of devils. They were made six thousand years ago; they were made to rule for six thousand years and their time expired in the year 1914. The only reason **GOD** didn't remove them then was because you and I were here in their clutches and God gave them an extension of time – not them an extension of time, but they received an extension of time to give the **wise men** of the East the opportunity to get into this "House of Bondage" and "awaken" the **"Lost Sheep."** Once the American so-called Negroes [Nubian Americans] have been awakened to a **"knowledge"** of themselves and of their own God and of the white man, then they're on their own. [Like what you're understanding reading here, that's known to Nubian Americans scattered across this nation.]

Then it'll be left up to you me whether we want to integrate we'll be destroyed along with them. If we **"separate"** then we have a chance for salvation. So on that note, in the name of **ALLAH,** and His Messenger the Honorable Elijah Muhammad, I bring my talk to a close, **"As-Salaam Alaikum."**

Which brings us to today, and our current dilemma. Sometime after the European "middle-ages," but perhaps most likely before, the white man created **"racism,"** a system whereby they started to denigrate the black man and instituted a system of dangerous ill-treatment, to death with extreme hate towards all black peoples. Many theorize that this is a direct result of ancient memories of the way the black man treated the white man, when the white man were termed Albinos, having to cross the hot sands of the Arabian Desert six thousand years ago in chains, naked except for an apron loincloth. A treatment perhaps necessary but was a most foul a torture indeed, whether deserved by their destructive trouble-making or not, it was done to the white man by the black man.

However, white man's destructive atrocities even to death, was over one hundred million with slaveries dead of men, women, and children many white historian scholar's theorize was to **en**sure, the black man would not one day become resurgent, anticipate, and return the killing favor to them. But this isn't about "tit-for-tat." More important is the **Mecca Prophecy.** Give me the black man's Nubian Messiah's, six thousand years prophecy white man to rule, until notified something **remotely** (controlled from a distance) outstandingly different, with God, that ain't.

The righteous Laws of GOD [ALLAH, the **Islamic** word for God] will control the reins of evil Lucifer's antichrist Trump's, devil followers, and their racist and corrupt Satan's mentality blood-lines, will surely die within the blink of an eye. A prophesized white man's conspiracy. A white man's rule of 6,000 years he knows is up. Against a black man's justified Hebrew **"Brotherhood."** Original HEBREW, **"Nubian/Ethiopian Jews,** are known as the "Beta Israel" is still today's havoc having a white man's **genocide** towards the **Palestinian** people, in their own **Israel** homeland, by **"European-Fake Jews."** Are the Jews illegally trying to steal all the land of Israel, regardless of others ownership? YES they are?

Why is there a need to **"rob"** the black man of his great and accomplished history, by the white man, and Euro-fake Jews? Is it because if he doesn't, everything the white man has ever done and accomplished is all behind whatever the black man did, built, high-technology, or in academics the white man learned to do, if you think about it, he has to look-up to which is only black man's just due. This is why white people looks down on in hateful envy; and his movies **"undermine,"** by **"whitewashing"** almost all **creations** and astounding **achievements** of the ancient great scientific black man; with his richest in natural resources continent on Earth, **AFRICA.** It sends the wrong message seeing only white movie actors, always playing all of black man's vitally important history, that's for educating children and future black generations.

America, is the beginner student in the worlds, **"school-house of Africa's learning."** Africa, once called the **"dark continent,"** the white man is trying little by little no matter how subtle, trying to make civilized Africa whitewashed. Viewing all of history text as falsely white including Biblical depictions of characters as white must end today is the dire essential necessity **"fight"** argued here and not even a hopeful promise of change by the white man. Whose never been fair or decent in all of history, just ask if we could **"Jim Crow"** era of the black man, the **"Apartheid"** era of Africa's black man, and today's **"Genocide"** of black and brown innocent and humble Palestinians!

All this amounts to, is a humiliating system of the black man's **"cultural assassination"** for elimination, that blacks on the other hand have never shown no need for towards the white man in history. Perhaps another major reason the white man hates the black man so is the **"terrible-way"** of their "characteristic inbred- trait of **hate**," towards black peoples, Yakub, their never new or saw black god, he had to do, with the "killing of black and babies of color," to create them. But never have the black man had an **incentive** nor an **objective** to do to them, like what the white man of oppression, do to black people.

Scientific **constraint** (repression of one's natural feelings), is needed of the white man's Adam and Eve, who appeared no more recently than **6,000 years ago,** on this Earth. Has nothing to say or argue about, with the black man's Adam and Eve on this Earth older than **"300,000 years ago."** Modern humans out of **Africa** was originally the first who settled in **Europe "40,000 years ago."** Data also confirms, that about **"8,500 years ago,** early hunter-gatherers in **Spain**, Luxembourg **Germany**, and **Hungary** also had dark to black skin.

In the far north, southern **Sweden** had light skin gene variants. They also had a third gene, HERC2/OCA2, which causes blue eyes and may have also contributed to light skin and blond hair. Hence, ancient hunter-gathers of the far north were pale and blue eyed. Those of Central Europe and Southern Europe, had much darker skin. Then, the first farmers from the **"Near East"** (southwest Asia, refers to Turkey, Lebanon, Syria, Iraq, Israel, and Saudi Arabia [so-called Middle East]), arrived in Europe and interbred with black, dark, and light skin indigenous hunter-gathers so that central and southern Europeans also began to have lighter skin.

Understanding is difficult, in a world without clear examples, from past histories trial and errors, of researches investigations to rely on and go by. However, the prestigious *"National Geographic Society"* has reported that scientists studying **"DNA,"** have now confirmed that "Europeans as a white man's people, are younger than we thought." Prof. Alan Cooper, director of the Australian Central for Ancient DNA, at the University of Adelaide, analyzed DNA from ancient skeletons and found that the **genetic** makeup of modern Europe (white man), was established the remarkable **"6,600 years ago,"** the exact date taught of a grafting process on an Island called **"Patmos"** (or Pelan), in the Aegean Sea, where they had been **"made"** by a 600 year process of selective breeding called **"grafting."**

On the island, a system of mating was based on skin color, in which only lighter-complexioned babies were allowed to survive. Over many generations the population of Patmos began to grow lighter and lighter until after **"600 years,"** the people became very pale with blue eyes and blond hair. From this island-based tribe of white skinned **"albinos"** came a behaviorally, [they seem a more concentrated evil type], aggressive race of rulers – namely the **"Caucasians,"** who now represent 9% of the world's population which is **"1 in every 11 human beings."**

Scientists have now overcome any controversy of time-span with **"proof,"** no longer a secret mystery the white species on Earth; is only **"6,000 years old!"** Other white folks are kidding themselves, framing their answers with confusing, abstract rhetoric and eluding the one fact missing, is the hidden 6,000 years ago **"creation"** without a doubt, their short history on earth and the black species beginning is the coming of all others. We the father, they the son, **"Mason."** Be aware, the mark of the beast's number is **"666,"** and America's first <u>terrorist</u> was the **"KKK!"**

Just as its hog's-wash logic no doubt being false, that the white man could not progress to his fullest potential if they were always looking up to the black man as personification, of knowledge, wisdom and advanced with ancient technology. <u>Racist</u> whites should "<u>hate</u> their game" and not the black man player's knowledge of it all, with his people having a much deeper devotion to **"God and His Laws of salvation,"** as no other race of people we know of here!

Whatever his white man's reason, not only resulted in cruel mistreatment of black people. But wrong and the way the white man's devious mentality is of not writing the black man Sudan's Nubian/Ethiopia great history, is left out of their writing of history is criminal. It's a pathetic thing to humanity to want to do. But is exactly what the white man has been going for **"centuries."** Scrupulous white man's academics of education, and an industry of people making <u>fake</u> "white looking" whitewashed from black artifacts and Nubian /Egyptian paintings, done to support their false and lies in history.

Not to mention the white man depicting him as the builder of the great pyramids of Gaza. And the white man's defacing, chipping away the wide nose and thick lips of the **Sphinx** recognizable as the black man. The white man tries to make it difficult to determine race in spiteful envy as they <u>steal</u> as their own, is a "matter of fact" <u>conspiracy</u> with Euro-Jews to write, to support theirs, excluding with <u>theft</u> of black man's out of **"his history"**... Will end with Nubian American's "whole-truth." A rare wine **"mellows"** with age. The truth in history is good. History that's good mellows in time better, as <u>lies</u> and <u>whitewashed</u> history historian scholars will fall in the **"<u>bottomless pit</u>."** Do not be **blunt** (dull) in representing, **Nubian Americans,** use **"tact,"** but plan going straight for the jugular. Know **how** to keep a good relationship with others with **"respect,"** based on a **keen instinct,** *"for"* a deserver, but always carrying a **"big stick!**

Since the black man has been free, from 400 years of slavery slowly, but critically are we really progressing **"depicting history,"** as a black race of Nubian Americans? No. So far, we now have at Christmas time a fiction black "Santa Claus," and a black "Bar-Bi-Doll." But how long is it gonna take, if ever, to get to show the original black baby Jesus Christ. A Nubian wooly-hair for Christmas, true Christ baby shown everywhere whose correct skin was black in color; and not the false white skin color shown everywhere. "Scared" and fear the **truth** white man?

By no stretch of the imagination, can you deny a black Jesus Christ with black nappy-hair, dark to black skin, dark brown eyes compared to a fiction, false, whitewashed with blond-straight haired, from dark brown to blue eyes, pale skin lie; to be accepted by white people, and this goes as **"true..."** What an ancient artist **Michael Angelo** seem to have started portraying a white man Christ, should have stayed with him, an Italian to pray to in Rome! Asks the question, why did the white man chose to pick in all of black man's history, a Nubian blackman **Jesus Christ** to whitewash??? Christ was an **activist-liberator** for black people. He was a renowned Black Man.

Also, when do we get our black pyramids back always per-trade with the white man, as if he built them, depicts a great lie. And the rest of black man's great and amazing history must be written in school text books. And don't ever forget white man, the respect that doesn't need asking, of the **"mother"** of every species on Earth; is the nappy-hair, big pretty behinds, breasts and an unmatched intellect is the black woman, whose the original first ever, **"QUEEN"** on Earth.

Black people must remember white politics promise to do, play of words like, "You **should** have power to insure empowerment," is a maybe instead of a backing with saying, "You **will** have power..." Does history repeat itself, as a universal law? Is the white man at war within himself Euro nations, and the Asiatic- Euro- Jews at the same time today? Is this fulfilling God's (Allah) black man's Islamic prophecy records, stored in Mecca; white man's last days down fall of world-rule; before black man's world-rule again, since his **"prehistory,"? YES!** All praises are due Allah, and in Christianity God bless us all with His soon, 1,000 years peace, on earth...

Before winding up in conclusion, the following must be said, that Islam was brought to the United States by enslaved African Muslims, and it retained a real presence in the country though small, was throughout the 19th century. It reemerged at the beginning of the 20th century as a result of the efforts of the Ahmadiyyah movement, an unorthodox sect founded in India by Mira Ghulam Ahmad (1839-1908), and of Shaikh Ahmed Faisal (1891-1980), the Moroccan-born leader of an independent Black Muslim Movement. Muslim teachings were tied to Black Nationalism by Noble Drew Ali, originally Timothy Drew (1886-1929), who founded the Moorish Science Temple of America in Newark, New Jersey in 1913. He produced a new sacred text, *The Holy Koran* that bears little resemblance to its namesake and was based on his limited knowledge of Islam and on spiritualist teachings.

Also known as the prophet, Drew Ali taught that all blacks were of Moorish origins but had their Muslim identity, to which today's DNA has proven of Nubian identity heritage origin, taken away from them through slavery and racist segregation. Populist and scientific racism identified all black Africans as primitive, or closer to **"apes,"** whites drew criticisms of white supremacist **Nordicism**, creating a mythic version of Anglo Saxon lineage and behavior voiced by black thinkers, is so pervasive in black racial thought to the "grafted devils." Conspiring against Nubian black man of Kush, with all white Biblical characters, and unscrupulous white,

Euro-Jew Zionist monsters of Satan's synagogue, Hebrews. Jesus Christ said of Satan (Rev. 2:9).

Cunning, deceitful and cowardly white historians, like displaying in hate, in retaliation or vengeance their crime, behind our selective breeding or graftation creating them; with depicting all white Biblical characters of black Africa, "Caucasian," even angles, to spite with great lies. Has been criticized as racist and pseudoscientific, with no historical or scientific evidence to support them. These depictions are metaphysical lies of history and origin. Pictures in the visual arts are all wrong, and an insult to the Bible, and innocent white people, ignorant of this visual lying art, that should be **"black and brown"** skin-color characters, pictures of **"Bible truth."**

The white guilty-conscience, perhaps, may seem to wish and dred, the secret **cover-up** of his creation, was never told by Islam. The terms black man, brown man, red man, yellow man, and white man are rooted in underline racist and dehumanizing, stereotypes, developed in the Caucasian Middle Ages, 15th century Western world; to denigrate, and marginalize people. Also, is based on flawed and harmful assumptions about race and "white supremacy" groups.

The creation of Adam and Eve, is described in the Bible, specifically in the book Genesis. While there is no exact date given, some [white man] interpretations suggest their creation [were white male and female], occurred roughly 6,000 years ago based on the white man's Biblical genealogies. Which place the emergence of modern like black man and woman much earlier, around 300,000 to 2 million years ago. How many years passed from Adam to now? The white man claims: from Adam to today, according to the Biblical timeline [which is a white man's manufactured deceptive lies, it has only been **approximately 6,000 years** is interesting, ridiculous. This time-span is not what the inspiring, but the devious white man manufactured, an unbelievable lie and outrageous.

When you say history, you look at the black race, then the others. The bizarre bullying and horrible take-over of black man's history, we blacks need to get our "illustrate history-building" arms around; and change, because Euro-Westerners distort the truth of life, to their advantage.

Euro-Western world researchers agree, our immediate ancestors, the upright walking **apes,** arose in **Africa.** But the discovery of a new primate that lived about 37 million years ago in the ancient swamplands of Myanmar bolsters the idea that the deep primate family tree that gave rise to humans is rooted in **Asia,** to which black historians rightfully in truth, beg to differ.

But if the above was true, then who are the Chinese descended from? Studies of Chinese populations show that 97.4% of their genetic make-up is from ancestral modern humans from **Africa,** with the rest coming from perhaps, extinct forms such as Neanderthals and Denisvans. July 13, 2016 – science AAAS. Seems, the white man "wants his cake and eat it too," with his conflicting damaging racist statement of Africa with mockery to him, an amusing "ape-black man." Contradicts known Africa being the **"cradle of civilization,"** is now, supposedly in Asia. But made clear the Chinese are a descendant from Africa's **ape,** shows the deep in his nature hate, he holds towards the scattered black Nubian African, Nubian American and all other races in his only 6,000 years existence!!!

Modern Homo-Sapiens people, migrated from Africa into the southern part of China around 60,000 years ago. All people today came out of **Babel** (Genesis 10:32). Do all humans have African DNA? Yes the percentage of African ancestry is relatively low, with the majority having just 0.5 percent to 0.75 percent. Everything said here is in the interest of justice…and not a "Lying of truth," to deceive and fool a lot of blacks, but mostly white people in order to rule the world, as was the black prophecy-records explain. Along with his creation records, stored in the Holy City of Mecca.

What was so important, that it totally surprised Malcolm X, visit to the Holy City of **Mecca?** During the seven days of this holy pilgrimage, while under the rituals of the Hajj [pilgrimage]. Malcolm X's first time in Mecca, he was sincerely shocked and surprised by the lack of racial division he expected, and the emphasis on unity and brotherhood he witnessed during his first pilgrimage to Mecca in 1964. He had previously been exposed to the Nation of Islam's ideology. It viewed white people as inherently evil, but his experience in Mecca [somewhat] challenged that perspective.

Malcolm X noted that Muslims of all colors, races, and nationalities were treated with respect and kindness, participating in religious rituals together, and showing genuine warmth towards each other. This was in stark contrast to the racial segregation he had experienced in the United States. Here is Malcolm X's letter from Mecca (April 20, 1964). Never have I witness such sincere brotherhood as practiced by people of all colors and races here in this Ancient Holy Land, the home of Abraham, Muhammad and all other prophets of the Holy Scriptures. For the past week, I have been utterly speechless and spell bound by the graciousness I see displayed all around me by people of all colors.

I have been blessed to visit the Holy City of Mecca. I have made my seven circuits around the Ka'ba, led by a young Mutawaf named Muhammad. I drank water from the well of Zem Zem. I ran seven time back and forth between the hills of Mt. Al Safa and Al-Marwah. I have prayed in the ancient city of Mina, and I have prayed on Mt. Arafat. There were tens of thousands of pilgrims, from all over the world. They were of all colors, from blue-eyed blonds to black skin Africans. But we were all participating in the rituals, displaying a spirit of unity and brotherhood that my experience in America had led me to believe never could exist between the white and non-white. America needs to understand Islam, because this is one religion that erases from its society the race problem.

Throughout my travels in the Muslim world, I have met, talked to, and even eaten with people who in America would have considered 'white'-but the 'white' attitude was removed from their minds by the religion of Islam. I have never before seen sincere and true brotherhood practiced by all colors together, irrespective of their color. You may be shocked by these words coming from me. But on this pilgrimage, what I have seen, and experienced, has forced me to re-arrange much of my thought patterns previously held, and to toss aside some of my previous conclusions. This was not too difficult for me. Despite my firm convictions, I have always been a man who tried to face facts, and to accept the reality of life as a new experience and knowledge unfolds it. I have always kept an open mind, which is necessary to the flexibility that must go hand in hand with every form of intelligent search for truth.

During the past eleven days here in the Muslim world, I have eaten from the same plate, drank from the same glass, and slept in the same bed, (or on the same rug)—while praying to the same God—with fellow Muslims, whose eyes were the bluest of blue, whose hair was the blondest of blond, and whose skin was the whitest of white. And in the same words and in the actions and deeds of the 'white' Muslims, I felt the same sincerity that I felt among the black African Muslims of Nigeria, Sudan and Ghana.

We were truly all the same (brothers)—because their belief in one God had removed the 'white' from their minds, the 'white' from their behavior, and the 'white' man from their attitude. I could see from this, that perhaps if white Americans could accept the Oneness of God, then perhaps, too, they could accept in reality the Oneness of Man—and cease to measure, and hinder, and harm others in terms of their differences in color. With racism plaguing America like an incurable cancer, the so-called 'Christian' white American heart should be more receptive to a proven solution to such a destructive problem. Perhaps it could be in time to save America from imminent disaster—the same destruction brought upon Germany by racism that eventually destroyed the Germans themselves.

Each hour here in the Holy Land enables me to have greater spiritual insights into what is happening in America between black and white. The American Negro here can be blamed for his animosities—he is only reacting to four hundred years of conscious racism of the American whites. But as racism leads America up the suicide path, I do believe, from the experiences that I have had with them, that the whites of the younger generation, in the colleges and universities, will see the hand writing on the wall and many of them will turn to the spiritual path of truth—the only way left to America to ward off the disaster that racism inevitable must lead to.

Never have I been so highly honored. Never have I been made to feel more humble and unworthy. Who would believe the blessings that have been heaped upon an American Negro? A few nights ago, a man who would be called in America a 'white' man, a United Nations diplomat, an ambassador, a companion of kings, gave me his hotel suite, his bed. By this man, His Excellency Prince Faisal who rules this Holy Land, was made aware of my presence here in Jedda. The very next morning, Prince Faisal's son, in person, informed me that by the will and decree of his esteemed father, I was to be a State Guest. The deputy Chief of Protocol himself took me before the Hajj Court. His Holiness Sheikh Muhammad Harkon himself okayed my visit to Mecca. His Holiness gave me two books on Islam, with his personal seal and autograph, and told me that he prayed that I would be a successful preacher of Islam in America.

A car, a driver, and a guide, have been placed at my disposal, making it possible for me to travel about this Holy Land almost at will. The government provides air conditioned quarters and servants in each city that I visit. Never would I have even thought of dreaming that I would ever be a recipient of such honors—honors that in America would be bestowed upon a king—not a Negro. All praises is due to Allah, the Lord of all the Worlds.

Sincerely, El-Hajj Malik El-Shabazz (Malcolm X)

["When said, **World-History,** you think of Africa's black race first, then all the others." "Don't do to my family, what you don't want done to yours, I won't do to you, is Godly."(The author)]

****

CHAPTER 4
Identity Identifying Lesson of Lessons

Belief, that black people created white people with "selected-breeding" in exclusion, perhaps is not mainstream belief within Judaism, does suggest there are some who does. Just like, black people are thought primate and too stupid to see through white supremacist or anti-Semite Euro-Jew schemes, to pose a threat to their kind, but poses a disastrous threat to democracy in America. Just like, the great Replacement Theory, is what black folks need to know just what Euro-Jews fear about white supremacy.

Just right before, a car, fatally plowed into protesters, near a "Unit the Right" rally, August 2017, neo-Nazi chanted "Jews will not replace us." Took place in Charlottesville. Also known as the white replacement theory and white genocide theory. A conspiracy theory, based on and rooted in white supremacist ideology, claims there is an international effort, led by Euro-Jews to promote mass immigration, intermarriage, and other efforts that would lead to the "extinction of whites." Accuse Jews of believing they are superior because they call themselves "God's Chosen People." Jews are a primary target of a white supremacist movement.

"It's those anti-Semitic tropes that Euro-Jews are manipulative and controlling and hold the power," said Natalia Mahmud, AJC Associate Director of U.S. Muslim-Jewish Relations. That black people is the tool used by Euro-Jews to unseat the white race from the proverbial, throne. An Islam prophecy of a true race creation that sounds almost unbelievable, hard to believe the truth, kept from you for four hundred years. White supremacist are troubled by the growing diversity of elected officials. Use anti-black protests as tools, to divide black folk from white and Euro-Jews.

The fact of the matter. There's a labeling of black supremacist. When they in reality, actually are civil-rights activists or black historians of **truth.** While Euro-Jews falsely claim to be "God's Chosen People." Proves they are not, is when they denounce ever being in <u>slavery</u>. The Biblical Exodus were black <u>slaves</u> that black Moses, led from Egypt. Doesn't support Euro-Jews white skin color **"<u>lie</u>"** a journey they claim made, called "The Exodus" is false. The "artistic-license"—for "Hollywood," gives a wrong permission right-away, allowing them to do this. Denies our black people's, just due by law. Has to be condemned! Confuses our children's learning, taught.

While, black people **<u>die</u>** significantly. Direct and indirectly with political procrastination-jive with a "stop and frisk law." From the bad, not the good police, than any other race of innocent people. And still, since Mr. George Floyd's <u>murder</u> by them 5 years ago 2020, in Minneapolis. **Accountability** is always finalized, with "<u>fake promises</u>," example: should have, would have, will have, and a tailored can be, only, **"if..."** If is a big word, mom used to say. No, stops directly or further, a sentence, or excuses with <u>lies</u>.

Just as today with Trump in office again, his "mandates" war, seems is to "roll-back," and is <u>dangerous</u> against democracy's, **"We the People."** Mandate (1: an authoritative command 2: an authorization to act given to a representative). Trump is <u>dictatorial</u>, and <u>criminalizing</u> mandates and its use as president of the United States of America! Trump is a wake-up call, never before seen here in America must end. **Needless loss of lives!** He's alarmingly desperate for a child-like attention. That's a selfishness, <u>cruel</u>, with **no-empathy** for <u>suffering</u> and <u>pain</u>. Crushing others, is "his attention." Example, like his name Trump, written on buildings, he doesn't own.

RESPECT, your race-created-genetic "Mother and Father." If you're not an Ashkenazi Jew, Mr. President. Deserves "honor" to know the truth, even if it hurts not with <u>hate</u>. Nubian black folk!

Black people were <u>abused</u>, and have been systematically oppressed by white America. Were exploited mentally, physically and sexually. Because of slavery and the Euro-Jewish Holocaust Nazi regime in Germany, millions of innocent people lost their lives, behind their race of skin color or religion. Later, created a huge almost, out of hand turmoil, in the 1960's "so violent and so extreme." America has voted in office a second term Trump, said would be a dictator his first day in office. What is America blatantly coming too? Read the hand writing on the wall!!!

Euro-Jew Zionists past and today made reputation, kills *them*. Today, Trump's poor and low-income cuts to Snap, health-care Medicaid, and Medicare are cruel, kills *us*, **We the People,** for the wealthy tax-cuts is flat-out, no-hold bars by him, wrong, against humanity and in America too! What's going on? *YOU*... Tax-cuts not needed to the "Ultra-Rich," their building "super-yachts" the length of a football field, capable with helicopters landing on deck! Unbelievable...

Our evaluation must contain **evidence** as well as **understanding** of the culture in question. There are so many things we can't and then can explain about ancient Nubian/ Egyptians giving our **opinion,** which in no way considered a **fact,** in writing history **"correctly."** Our personal opinions doesn't count, so we explain with proof/evidence always based on **"facts."** In fact, the problem is that modern day white scholar professors teaching in universities will the majority of the time simply go with, "We have **"no idea"** how blacks could have done this. Like if the white man couldn't figure it out how, how could the black man; instead of stating in reality, is brilliant of what the **"black man did do."** Staring him right in his bug-eyed, amazed face is the advance and high-technology of levitation. What he can't imitate he makes-up excuses, how it was not done, by the **"Nubian/Ethiopian/Egyptian black man!"**

With a pathetic theory of outer space aliens from another star-system, coming to help black men built what he couldn't by himself; is the perfect example of the white man's envious, hateful and bias

<u>racism</u> towards the black man and people of color.

The sensitivity level is high of the black man, because of the disrespect the white man seems to think he's far superior to the black man; when the white man was **"given"** his time to rule, not anything he done to dare claim superiority over black and brown people; especially the sacred **"ancient black gods,"** who once ruled worldwide. Because if space aliens were buddies with blacks, they would have kept their black friends from going into **"<u>slavery</u>,"** them being superior over everybody, doesn't makes sense of the space-alien theory.

And again, the white man always <u>omitting</u> the ancient **Sudan** history of **Nubia,** if Egypt was **responsible** for science, math, astronomy, technical engineering, the use of electric power etc. why not give credit to them having advanced to the knowledge into having **nuclear isotopes,** evidence left behind all indicate. However, without our knowledge of nuclear power at the time of writing, wouldn't have recognized, much less the science of **"flight,"** within and outside our atmosphere. Ethiopian **grandmother,** Nubian the **mother,** and Egyptian is the **child** of history.

They say, "There's nothing **NEW** under the sun," no doubt. <u>Whitewashing</u> to substantiate their white culture over the black man's culture. It was left up to **"<u>reinventing</u> Caucasians,"** thinking themselves clever, that if, it wasn't them to have done something astounding, to give credit only to some form of outside Earth's assistants; hence, TVs History Discovery channel's Space Alien, all <u>fiction</u> <u>opinions</u>. They try to prove in <u>fiction</u>, and <u>speculation</u> disregarding the fact of reality what black men didn't do, but what the black man indeed did, all by himself!!!

We can't explain a lot of things we see remaining in Egypt, because we refuse to open our minds to things that today could possibly **explain** them. For instance, in ancient stone a sign, with a helicopter, flying saucer, and submarine look a likes over the entrance of the magnificent temple of **Seti I** at **Abydos,** or the **Saqqara Bird** (spaceship?), and one of the artifacts called **Gold Flyers** found in **Columbia.** All this asks a question, when was the scientific revolution a **"distinction of Africa?"**

This brings to mind, what is the thinking of the, **"scientific method?"** To discover cause and effect relationships by asking questions, carefully gathering and examining the evidence, and seeing if all the available information can be combined into a logical answer. Keep in mind that new information or thinking might a scientist to back up and repeat steps is called an iterative process. The question, research, hypothesis, experiment, procedure, conclusions and results:

- Step 3 – Hypothesis. Educated guess or prediction of the outcome experiment.
- Step 4 – Experiment. Test the hypothesis.
- Step 5 – Data collected...
- Step 6 – Results/Conclusion.
- Step 7 – Communicate.

The **"Scientific Revolution,"** is traditionally held by most Caucasian historians began in **1543,** when the books De humani corporis fabria (On the working of the Human Body) and also De Revolutionibus, by the astronomer Nicolaus Copernicus, were first printed.

Civilization does not mean it contains or needs any <u>judgement of value</u>. Because if the judges are only Caucasian or Euro-Jew white scholars, historians or archeologists who determines who is worthy of **inclusion.** An incorrect "in the beginning," uncivilized ideology of Blacks with the exception of Egypt given the favor an admixture, which allowed **Semitic Nomads** (Caucasian looking) progression into black man civilized first civilizations, is complete <u>racist</u> fantasy claims as: true history. Could be true if, the depipctured white, was **"reversed."** Semite (whites) perhaps meaning, a more concentrated-<u>lack</u> of skin-color, rhythm and cold of empathy, and love but full of <u>hate</u> suppressed, and in your face **"smiling"** to function unnoticed, except in wrong deeds that surface makes it perfectly clear.

Is genetically a trait readily to war and danger is the Semite. Instead of the **Nubian/Kemite** (original name of Egypt before the Greek's naming) guest for peace and tranquility, not war and strife of a Semitic's, whites nature inclined to war? However, early civilization societies dealings with trade, left clues of written records, artifacts and archeological evidence we can analyze to rightly narrate our past, also includes those preserving their histories orally. Between about **4,000** and **3,000 BC,** white civilizations emerged. In the fertile river valleys of **Mesopotamia** and **Northeast Africa** this book with proof/evidence begs to differ, is false by the white man trying to fit in, is off by thousands of years by **black man's** true, accurate calculations of **"pre-history."**

Today, they will try to tell you that **Israel** is not part of Africa that once was, but behind the white man's manipulation that it is now, part of **Asia.** He plans to steal all of it as white man's territory. However the Bible clearly says that before the land was called Israel, it was called the land, **Canaan.** Read: Genesis 17:8. Canaan was the son of **Ham** (Father of the Africans) therefore Israel was at one point part of the land of ham (Africa), according to scripture. Also (at one time) included was part of the so-called Middle East, where the children of **Ishmael** (Arabs) now live.

In ancient **Savanna,** what's now Northwestern **Morocco, Africa,** and with the examination of fire-baked tools suggest these black people lived more than **300,000** to **350,000 years ago,** twice as old as previously thought. Fill a gap in **"the human fossil record."** Because, these people bear striking similarities to **modern** humans, lived well before the older fossil evidence **Homo-sapiens.**

Is a site in **Ethiopia,** dated about **195,000 years ago** of African in origin. Paleoanthropologist, in **2007** studied. Well dated African fossil sites, containing modern humans and their precursors (forerunners).

Africa, during her **"Flourishing Green Sahara"** periodic events, humans dispersed widely across the continent. It cannot precisely be said, where the black man evolved on the continent. African historians wrote, **Akebu-Lan** is the oldest and means "Mother of Mankind." **Ethiopia,** the *"Garden of Eden"* identity, was used by black Moors, Nubians, Numidians, Khart-Haddans (Carthagenians). The name Africa, was given to the continent by the Romans. During this time in **1,675 BC,** neither name "Jew" nor "Negro" existed. **Jealousy,** is why the white man always wants to question as if it didn't happen, just because the black man written it, when actually Africa did flourish in black man advanced technology, empowered **"Nubian's green Sahara."**

Once called the "Dark Continent" by the white man, he also agrees is the history of creation, humanities, and civilization all began in Africa. However, three major factors seem to try and obscure these vital **facts:**

1. Africa is an immensely large continent. The largest in the world, has been in constant **flux,** a continuous change of invasion, colonization, and apartheid and incorporated with what was written solely by **Europeans** point of view. Black people never believe what they hear from the white man as they do from their own kind, with back-up of scriptures Biblical and the Koran.
2. The history is complicated by a predominance of oral history handed down and massive destructions of black man's libraries and documents not hidden. Europeans as Romans in **45 BC** and **Christians** in 389 AD, much of black man's history was lost when the **"Library of Alexandria"** was destroyed.
3. The most important to remember: the European conquest of Africa which attempted to attribute all important achievements of the black man as Caucasians. Like Marie La Veau said, "Don't ever let someone else tell your history. They don't know it, so they tell it the way they want it to be, not the way it really was. Sometimes they even push you out of you history and claim it for themselves.

4. Nubian caravans crossed the Sinai Desert **6,000 years ago** to trade **"gold"** even as far away as **China,** from the valley of the Nile. Shortly before 3,000 BC Palestine and Syria were closely linked by excellent trade routes to Nubia. Egypt and Babylonia and during this era is believed even by **Semite** historians, that's black man's beginning of **"recorded history."**

Black man Abraham, began the traditional Biblical history of the first black **Israelite Jew,** (And not the later on, so-called white Euro-Jew by claiming converting to Hebrew religiously lack being of "bloodline," that only "confirms" being of the Hebrew origin), by leading his people out of **Ur,** his homeland in Southern **Mesopotamia** to eventually settle in **Canaan,** later called **Palestine.** According to black man **Hebrew** tradition, before leaving Ur, Abraham taught his followers the existence of one God, and rejected idol-worship and sins of Ur. Black Jews recognize God and His covenant with Abraham, indicating their special relationship remains one of the most important aspects of the black man's Jewish faith.

Tradition reports of several generations later, Abraham's grandson **Jacob** (also called **Israel** by God) had 12 sons, who became the ancestors' of the **"Twelve Tribes of Israel."** They also describe the transition to monotheism and the covenant relationship between God, and "the children of Israel."

One of these twelve sons, **Joseph,** led followers from Canaan during a famine to settle in Egypt. Biblical text by design, describe the Israelites were black, prosperous and becoming powerful, having only the Nubian/Egyptian **Pharaoh** to fear their influence. To stem the black Israelite then, the pharaoh tried putting harsh restrictions on births and forced them into slave labor, like todays white Israeli criminal influence against the **Palestinians.**

Back then with the Pharaoh, a black man **Moses,** whose mother right after birth had secreted him away in a waterproof basket on the **Nile River,** played an important role in delivering his people from subjugation (defeat of enslavement). He was like a modern-day, Harriet Tubman's **"Underground Railroad."** According to black man Hebrew tradition, God tasked Moses with leading his people out of Egypt a flight to freedom was a **"Black Called Exodus"** of world history.

Moses and the Israelites **"walked"** from Egypt back home to Israel. About **300 miles** was   Africa at the time. This is before the white man built the **"Suez Canal,"** putting Israel separating conveniently to steal with their influence in **Asia**. Another fact to ponder, the poor choice if Mary with baby Jesus Christ were "white skin" and fled into an all, "black skinned community" in Egypt avoiding the **Roman** King Herod's raft their contrast of white against black would have stood out like a "sore thumb;" and gotten them caught by his searching party!

Black man Moses led his "children of Israel" into **Sinai,** where they entered into the Sinai Covenant. This covenant bound all Israelites as today's nationalities of all colors and creed must love one another into a religious pact house of worship, to all mighty God. And not to desecrate or violate the Black Hebrew bloodline people's culture to which, the so-called white man Euro-Jew has done just that falsely claiming to be Hebrew by worshipping… His house of a **"love covenant."** Israelites agreed to worship God alone and obey His law, God confirmed the place of the Israelites as His **"Chosen People,"** were all black people there then, whom He would protect.

As part of the covenant, Israelites agreed to follow the **"Ten Commandments."** According to Hebrew scripture, God gave the Ten Commandments (actually there were 130 some odd or plus the ten) to the Israelites at **Mount Sinai,** instructing the Israelites to worship only Him, keep the Sabbath, **and honor their parents.** Even, to the "Let us make man parent blacks." The white man emphatically doesn't agree, only with hate to show for it. The Commandments among the many called the Ten, also prohibit idolatry, blasphemy, murder, adultery, theft, dishonesty, and coveting. These written accounts established important elements of the black man's **Jew** faith.

For example, Hebrew patriarchs: Abraham, Isaac, Israel (alternatively known as Jacob), and the twelve sons of Israel. **Israelites** (not Israeli Euro-Jews) believe in one God, Hebrew **Yahweh,** they perceived **Yah** (Yahweh) as being **just** and **merciful.**

In Hebrew, "Yah," is short for the divine name "Yahweh" (written as YHWH). Considered the personal name of God. In the Hebrew Bible, not Jesus, and "Yah" is a shortened form of "Yahweh," essentially referring to God as well; therefore neither "Yahweh" nor "Yah" represent Jesus. Jesus is not Yahweh even if some Christians believe he is. In translation of the Hebrew Bible into ancient Greek Lesous was used to represent the Hebrew/Aramaic name Yeshua, a derivation of earlier Hebrew Yehoshua, or Joshua. Jesus native Hebrew/Aramaic name was **"Yeshua."**

Another thing we'd like to make clear with the concerns of, "Let us make man," black rulers called gods. The "gods" of Psalm 82 is that earthly judges must act with impartiality and true justice, because even judges must stand someday before the judge. Psalm 82:6 and 7 warn human magistrates that they, too, must be judged: "I said 'You are gods; you are all sons of the Most High.' But you will die like mere men; you will fall like every other ruler." According to this view, God has appointed men to positions of authority in which they are considered as **"gods"** among the people. (See Exodus 7:1.)

The ideas that is but one universal God and that His laws apply to everyone have been defining tenets of other monotheistic religions. Subsequent written and oral traditions, like the **Talmud** reflect further development of white man's Euro-Jewish beliefs, ethics, laws and <u>white</u> <u>supremacy</u> practices. Out-right display of Israeli **"racism"** and non-infusion wanted by others.

After the Black Exodus, the Israelites resettled in Canaan, and in time began to **unify.** They formed **Kingdoms** in the **Levant** prior to **1,000 BC.** King **Saul** (1030-1009 BC), a member of one of the "Twelve Tribes of Israel," established the first Israelite monarchy, ruled over limited territory. Then he died not completely defeating his enemies nor unification. He was killed in battle with the **Philistines.** His son, King **David** (969 BC), established the United Kingdom of Israel, with its capital at **Jerusalem.** King David's successor, his son **Solomon,** further shaped the Kingdom. After the Exodus, during the unification, is where the Euro-Jews confusion comes in that's deceptive and with false narrative were not Europeans unifying.

Popular history tells of the biblical memory, that Kind David is remembered for defeating **Goliath.** Historical writings also celebrate him for expanding the boarders of a newly unified Israel, contributing to the Book of **Psalms,** and in Christian tradition, for being a forbear of **Jesus.** David began to build Jerusalem into the capital city of the Israelites, with further plan to build a **temple** to house the "Ark of the covenant" according to Hebrew tradition. Like Abraham, David is considered an important figure by **Jews, Christians,** and **Muslims.**

However, here is all the "identity evidence lessen put into a disproving authenticity of so-called Euro-Israeli Jews; who are fundamentally an imitation by imitating a black not white, **"legendary Hebrew culture."** The question **lies** do they have a **"moral"** right much less a **"legal"** right is **"criminal."** A wrongful foreign advantageous <u>occupation</u> of another peoples' land. Euro-Jews not only imitate but converting black man's history written down as his own after <u>invasion</u>. They created a reprehensible **persecution** to **Palestinians** after the **fact** is "double-jeopardy." Euro-Jews should be held accountable not being above the **"Law"** of the **"United Nations."** We for now, rest our case!

These <u>lies</u> do <u>harm</u> and <u>kills</u>! What doesn't kill you, makes you more **resilient** and **stronger** in your **"destiny."** And simply, in leaving, before we forget, just as thousands of miles of water doesn't separate **Hawaii** as not being a part of the **United States of America** and is not East **Asia;** is the same as saying the European man-made Suez Canal of narrow water doesn't separate **Israel** as not being a part of the **Northeast African continent** and is not West **Asia.** Just as Hawaii is part of **America's continent** prescribes in all due respect, the same as modern day **Israel** being as always in the past; an ancient United Kingdom, nations of **Northeast Africa's continent true identity!** Nubian Christ's identity homeland's **"Dark-continent"** they couldn't depict-white, but eventually claimed a white Christ in much lighter-skin people **Asia!** Learned tricknology of **Yakub.**

This is absolutely two ambiguously **right** ways of simple understanding; the white man is taking the opposite resolution to substantiate an ill-legit take all by force **Israeli Nation.** Certainly undermines any truth by them to go by for history. Black or White supremacy racism **won't fly!!!**

We desperately need, more Nubian Americans on the inside making important **"decisions,"** in congress. And don't forget brown **Latino's** brotherhood as well, together in congress politics. As black beautiful old folks we dearly miss would say, besides "there's nothing new under the sun," **"Dare jess ain't no telling,"** – "We really don't know to tell the truth, what kind of hi-tech possible mechanical, magnetic, nuclear, or black man's ancient Levitation science **"blue-prints"** were left behind. Prehistory tends to hint may still be around. Waiting to be discovered hidden, or buried.

Beneath the deep sands, **Nubian/Egyptian** lands perhaps. Destroyed or submerged under a white man's unnecessary created lake of water, recently done in Sudan's country of **Nubia,** its people protested against. We doubt very much "classified top-secret;" Euro-nations waiting a code to be solved **undeciphered hieroglyphics.** Dare jess **ain't** no telling, cause we way down under dah **son,** the black man!

This information is what all black and brown people need to know, not to be separated and divided by white man's history. Not what we want to hear and read from white man's written history. Because, **"the strength of honesty"** is here in black man history for "world brotherhood" that's vitally necessary. Understand the history of let us make man let the truth rise where it may.

Why not escalate equalization of **honest programing.** A program that reaches-out and teach a **moralistic** right-away, an **integrity** attitude of dignity, better understanding and mind-set that obey and honor like sons and daughters of "caring mothers and fathers," towards one another; "Let us make man." The **"Soul"** of culture is here within these pages, with a loud drum beat of black rhythm for peace, with love, happiness and **no-nonsense** warriors of **"Democracy."**

The mind-set for willing young and old warriors Nordic, Euro-Ashkenazi Jews, politicians and all white man police officers need to be "re-educated" with **"black historian text."** New to the many unknown **"identity text."** And new school **"Advanced Africa's World History,"** to correct the misinformation and misleading racist text heard about and have learned to know. A true mind-set that will start a positive movement almost all their masses will **conform** and **grow** into **"co-existing,"** knowledgeable and responsible **"caring people."** Is **reality** of it all counts.

Anyone thinking in a dictator mind-set, unscrupulously above the **law,** in the white house. With destruction of justice actions and their demonist policy tools, should go to jail in America, **regardless.**

Because all human rights of equality are on the table from our last election. With a said dictator wanna be. We the people, must be extra careful. To the most questionable and gullible, "History Channel Aliens," supposedly changing all history of the black man's great ancient accomplishments white advocates can't duplicate. Paraphrasing, they say **yes.** Their **"Ancient Astronauts Hypotheses,"** agree among themselves is mockery assumptions and pretension that are not logical. However, if there's anything of truth of what they say, it would be only **our own** black and brown ancient astronauts of our **solar-system** checking on us, monitoring their children (us) but keeping their distance and their secrets to themselves. Hits the nail on the head hear. But in truth, doubtful, also explained earlier. This book in its entirety doesn't imply any kind of hate, just **facts** of truth.

We will end this chapter with a portfolio of our other history texts. Changing of publisher hopefully books available soon: "A Child's Short History Book" – A Black History Month African Study in cartoon animal characters. "THE WORLD'S TRUE BLACK HISTORY – **FIRST EDITION.**" A FORTNEY ENCYCLICAL BLACK HISTORY. "THE AFRIAN CHRONOLOGIC HISTORY IS BIBLE – **SECOND EDITION**" *THE FORTNEY ENCYCLICAL WORLD HISTORY.* "THE NEW SCHOOL UNTOLD HISTORY – **THIRD EDITION**" *THE FORTNEY ENCYCLICAL HISTORY UNTOLD*, are precious. Make them your **"treasured"** family heirloom! **"Knowledge is Power."**

Today's white gods' rule, controls what the people think is real when it is not, is **"questioned"** and isn't dignified. Whereas, in pre-histories past, black gods' rule, controlled what the people thought was real, really was, dignified and was what the people **"knew."** We desperately need earnest and honest **"reform"** in world history education!

Today, education isn't talking about nor discussing a Nubian American's earnest, honest and dedicated long over-due put in place, reading text of their **Sudan, Nubia's** accomplished great history, in public schooling must be **"known."** Because by no stretch of the imagination can you deny a white Christ to be accepted by black folks when the scriptures describe Him, as a black man. Then you praying to a false-god white man, in darkness not knowing the truth… So why, what was the real reason, the white man chose a black Jesus Christ to whitewash? Or was it truly because Christ was a **Sudan Nubian,** like the **Nubian American Identity,** with wooly hair and black skin. The white man will not pray to a black man, who he made in evil-suffering a **slave!**

We are at the end, of starting a new beginning in these trying days and time of history, and "Let us make man" is valuable **"powerful knowledge,"** to learn, knowing of this **fact.** Was so delicately told and explained in Islam, but not in white man's Christianity is **"love teaching of truth"** with understanding, knowledge and wisdom and not <u>hate</u>. Perhaps why wooly haired black people wonder being attacked so much in our innocence, as God's chosen people. *The Fortney Encyclical History Ed. Co.* gets into scientifically researched truth, **"tells it like it is."** Written with proof/evidence that substantiate authenticity. Our noble aspiration that's humble but brave with courage is hoping, one day the news will report all U.S. public schools **"Advanced Nubian World history Studies,"** history curriculum that **shines** for our children and their children's future generations, from the pages of our history books, that our plane has landed.

All started out was finding what was being kept from us, what was the white man hiding from us first? Laid the foundation what **"<u>damages</u>"** and **"<u>harm</u>"** was done, **"<u>hidden</u> to defend."** Then brought into the **"light"** was exposing those who oppose the truth with no hesitation. Will sure enough save the world for a better **"co-existing."** Things happen in time, on time, and the right time to which God is good all the time. **YAH** man, it is you, godly like whose **reality** has always been the beginning of history. Starter of all civilizations, sprung from the family tree, motherland **Africa. "Hal-le-lu-jah!** "Ethiopia's Hebrew" has a parallel path with **Nubian**-Egyptology, where all praises are due in written history. Euro-Jews try to claim Hebrew as theirs, is the originator with all claims to the synagogue of **"Satan,"** Bible scripture validate. An **end** to anti-black <u>racism</u>.

THE <u>ALBINOS</u> MOST OUTRAGEOUS LIES

Slavery was NOT **"America's Original Sin,"** <u>GENOCIDE</u> was!!! Shows how <u>racist</u> and <u>evil</u> **terrorist** (KKK- Klu, Klux, klan) trouble-makers they are by hiding, Black People's whole true pre-history high-tech accomplishments before and after history, through educating a "<u>Jim Crow Era</u>" is an untrue <u>docile</u> form of Black

Genocide (murder). Was not the "superb black intellect" of black man's great history. Another of Albinos most outrageous lies is that, they are white-skinned because they are a "Cold Adapted People" who evolved white skin to better absorb sunlight for synthesis vitamin "D." It is a ridiculous lie, and thoroughly debunked scientifically. Most certainly fits the script, of all Yakub's tricknology learning; of "how to rule and govern for 6,000 years, before the **black man again**... Does Trump hide, ashamed being an **Ashkenazi**? Would lie being a white man, if knowing created by blacks? Or strangely both? Is questionable!

The Caucasian lie, feeds into an overall "lie **methodology**" used to keep Blacks ignorant and powerless. Is all part of a media, academia, and institutions lie, is their media of safety. Now, with no intentions here to hurt any ones feelings, we just present real truth and not pretending with lies and fantasy as real. Just as it should be understood, in learning that prior to or before 100,000 BC, and in Europe after the passing of the ice age or it had gone about 45,000 BC. The great flood was about 12,000 BC and the Caucasian creation was 6,600 years ago. Erroneously Albinos declared to be the European – the Black **Grimaldi** is known to be the first European.

The first civilization in the Caucuses was the **Colhian** culture. "Greek historian" **Herodotus** (440 BC) described the Colchians. **Quote:** "Egyptians said that they believed the Colchians to be descended from the army of Sesostries. My own conjectures (guesses) were founded, first on the fact that **they are black skinned and have wooly hair,** which certainly amounts to but little, since several other nations are so too; but future and more especially, on the circumstance that the Colchians, the Egyptians, and the Ethiopians (Nubians), are the only nations who have practiced circumcision from earliest times."

Before we go any further, lets first establish who truly the original or "real" first Caucasians were, will certainly be surprising. We begin with the clay sculpture portraying the face of the earliest known eastern European: made from the modern human skull of a Black person, constructed from fragments found in Pestera cu Oase, the "cave with bones," that's located in the southwestern Carpathian Mountains of Romania in 2002. The bones were carbon – dated to between 34,000 and 36,000 years ago.

Another of Albinos [the author, Anglo-Saxon Caucasian **Christians** mind you] outrageous lie, remind us to remember again the old saying once before Mari La Veau – "Don't ever let someone else tell your history. They don't know it, so they tell it the way they want it to be, not the way it really was. Sometimes they even push you out your history and claim it for themselves.

SAD BUT TRUE: We at Realhistoryww.com continually marvel at how apparently intelligent Black and people of color [would] swallow and believe whatever their best friend friends – the **Albinos** [author, and semi-white "Biblical described Satan" bigoted **Semite Euro Jews**] tell them. What you say? Who would be **stupid** enough to believe that the [same] people who **enslaved, murdered, lynched,** and relegated (COMMIT) them to **"second class"** citizenship [as a horse or cattle] would tell Blacks the **truth** about ANYTHING??? Well that's actually true – intelligent people would **"never believe them."** They act like we came from them…coming from us **Blacks!**

Trump is America's **"wake-up call,"** and to the world **God** don't like ugly! A liar can't be trusted. Especially one with a **mediator,** to **recognize** and **negotiate** a path for anything. Nubian Americans have over-paid in dues for **"respect,"** politically ignored even with protests. Nubian future **politicians** and **judges** (with backbones), the grand historian author says, "Go to bed early, early to rise, makes young blacks healthy, wealthy and wise. Beating them with "more numbers, and justice under God, and **His laws.** For "We the People." And please remember, **"Origin History,"** deeply affects **psychological behavior** and relates **self-esteem.** Stay strong, stay wise, always plan with **honesty** and have **"eyes"** also in the back of your head!!!

Our honorable intentions are for **"we the people."** We write and stress what the **"Root of Evil Is."** Only with facts, that explain "proof/evidence" to support understanding for all. And not taking **"No Mess,"** doing it! Is how it's done. By **action** denouncing "Historical **brain**-washing" "erasing and **white**-washing" Nubian Americans past. Blacks want to see **connecting** their past experiences and high-tech **pre-history** accomplishments accurately represented in **"mainstream"** history and **"society."** INSPIRING, honorably with dignity and integrity of traditions in **Nubian American** remembrance, historical interpretation, and **"activism."** What is "Superior"…? **Hah…**

Not depicted, lying white man copied black into "fiction history movies." Stand-up for true great black and people of color's proud, flourishing **"thoroughly researched phenomenal pre-history"** and history that **really matters,** "now and forever!" Is **outstanding,** not necessarily superior…

Because lawless, **"Authoritarian,"** is the principal of blind obedience attacks **"Democracy."** An authority not responsible to the people. Whose reasoning is the use of "terrorism" to repress, compel, and enforce, are the means of its, coercion. The freedoms of democracy depends on the constitution of basic laws is threaten by suffering cruelty of evil **Satanism** all-white "Christian Nationality" is Trump's authoritarian idea. **"Lying"** superior and doing what he said he wouldn't do. By denying aid to black and people of color, dismantle education and agencies that would secure the constitution, while taking those monies, **"loading his pockets."** However, with unity, is what "we the people" must stand together and fight will defeat, the enemy of DEMOCRACY.

World-wide observance is, 34 felon's Trump. Using if unaware, YAKUB'S "Tricknology." As anti-Semitism must stop its **own** anti-color de-humanism of black and brown people. Is murder, in Gaza, and Sudan racism, with suffering, starving, and merciless killings, denying USAID to the needy. All **needless** loss of life. Is almost unbelievable <u>horror</u> attack humans. "**<u>Satan's</u> <u>evil</u>.**"

NOTE: From Africa's Biblical truth, guiding, of Kush (Cush) until today's Nubian Americans *dramatic,* intellectuals, integrity, and inspiring people through-out all of history, empowerment comeback. Comes the light, will come new-day valuable discoveries advancing all nationalities. Which does away with most of <u>death</u>-dealing-<u>racism</u>. Is at hand renders unquestionable good! Closing the door, to Euro-Jew <u>Satan's</u> <u>evil</u>, running parallel too, Caucasian-white <u>devil's</u> <u>reign</u>!!!

Should futures next great two, world powers be unbelievable, Nubian American's homeland Africa's continent, largest country *Sudan,* and Asia's largest country *China* expertise combined. Like prehistory, "Gold Trade" of Nubians to the great Chinese people in China, **6,000 years ago.** It's in our Nubian **"nature."** It is black man's Nubian nature of do-good, to flourish. Who knows what else the future may hold that's fine, with promises of Islam and Christian "prophecy." As his's not the created "<u>trouble</u>-maker" by nature, *prophesized* white man. Good, Black & Yellow **"respect"** to show the world perhaps a prophecy of Mecca, not manifested as yet. Perhaps no longer blind now you see. A new order of **China** and **Africa rises,** with flourishing co-existence.

The end of the **"<u>devils</u> <u>reign</u>"** is close. The harder he fight blacks with <u>corrupt</u> **Jews** not satisfied his **ruling!** Low-income folks and the poor, top interest to live and advance seek funds. Needed in Urban communities. Trump is purposely leaving out funds for Nubian American children, vital for their Public Education **Schooling.** However, only by the **"saving"** grace of almighty God, the ultimate plan, and Mecca's **"Prophecy"** of **"Let Us Make Man,"** is now being fulfilled. Messiah, and the **Nubian** Jesus Christ, will help us win this <u>war</u> with "Law and the Constitution." God **"will surely"** bless us **obeying** Him with a "thousand years" **peace.** At last truth. Black man's history book is, the **"Holy Bible."** The Black man **wrote!** HE, will make a way. What YOU read here, **is right,** and about *"faith."*

Just believe. And, *AT LAST TRUTH*...

"AMERICA IS NOW CALLING EVIL...GOOD" *Isaiah 5:20.* There has been a gay parade in Israel's holy city of Jerusalem. A **Gay Pride Parade** in New York City was an abomination, and disgusting in God's sight. They also take to themselves the "right" to corrupt moral culture. Took place in New York, June of 2006.

From the very beginning "God condemns homosexual sodomites." Please read (Genesis 19:1-29; Roman 1:26-27; 1 Corinthians 6:9-10). The Bible teaches homosexuals and Lesbians are an abominations and sin against God. Those practice such are worthy of death and shall not enter the Kingdom of God. The natural and proper sexual relationship is a "man and woman" joined together as Husband and Wife" in marriage (God's Divine Institution – Genesis 1:27-28, 2:18-24; Psalms 127:3-5; Matthew 19:4-6). God did not make homosexuals; their actions are a result of their own lust and <u>evil</u> desires (James 1: 13-14). A "heterosexual" matrimony is a **sacred matter!**

The nerve to say I'll be a <u>dictator</u> on day one, and then won the election goes to show the many (60% perhaps <u>racist</u>) wanting an all-white America. Same sex marriage, is a law agreed with Trump should **ban,** an under-cover black **genocide** as law 10 years now, **should end.** Gay-rights to let-live will be protected. Trump's, political abuse, republican lying, cowards creating the poor getting poorer, the sick getting sicker, and dramatic increase in death, all for the 1% wealthy and *unneeded* **"tax-cut."** Whereas, many of 700 hospitals will close-down depriving the people, with cuts to Medicaid and Medicare of a **trillion plus dollars.** And we **"paying"** for it!!!

"Health-Care is a Right Not a Privilege." Funding Trump's budget-bill, effects the "Food – SNAP program" and hundreds of thousands of children lives! Nursing homes for the elderly! All Americans, besides targeting African nations deprived of life-saving **vaccines.** If passing of America's ever, largest tax-cut for the wealthy. For what? Buy their "super-yachts"? Democrats need 4 votes to win the Senate, in the House; over the Republicans, would foil the bill...

An attack is targeting black women, whereas 13 black women to every 1 white woman, are **dying**. Needing pregnancy help, with Obama's "healthcare," is denied in southern red states. This is black genocide in America at present, going on that, **must end.** All to void black **"votes."**

We here nailed why, a retaliation Caucasian hate problem created racism; that proves blacks created the white man, 6,000 years ago with religious evidence, he heinously resents. Regardless whatever said, this is a fair, short-time existing collection and correct assessment of **"His-story."** Here is an **"origin"** *precise* perspective of world history's family-tree, **"solved."** May save lives, with the knowledge gained and understood, from the information in this book. Our company is mindful how we express race and history. **Nubian** people of **Sudan** suffered. Losing to slavery; sons and daughters in the wilderness of America. Scattered world-wide. Whose perseverance, is like no other race. With their impact in history are phenomenal like no other! Deserve the **honor** of writing here, these amazing lessons of true facts with proof/evidence, Nubian Americans will return *"home"* soon, with a gift of **empowerment** to advance, **"AFRICA."** Again, now **our** time!

Dare Trump, as a "great **genius** U.S.A. hero," if taxing the wealthy **only** 4%, ending **poverty**! However, the democratic news pressure of the Epstein heinous child pedophile crimes, Trump fury association that resist a document list release. May perhaps overshadow selling the idea of a **"genius and hero"** of a 4% tax increase on the affordable wealthy...? Perhaps parallel to the deaths of innocent babies, to create a Mecca's prophesized white race!!!

Advance science or myth is there evidence of Mr. Yakub? The Honorable Minister Louis Farrakhan said, "When they make mockery of what God has revealed to the Honorable Elijah Muhammad, they say that Yakub was an evil scientist. Wrong! Yakub was a scientist who saw in the genetic makeup of the Black man that he could bring out of us a new people, the opposite of the original. That is not evil. That is high science."

The Ashkenazi Jew (or White Euro-Jews) have scrambled to create a diversion away from the unanswerable 512-page indictment by ridiculing the history of Yakub Islam relates. According to Mr. Elijah Muhammad is "exactly" when Mr. Yakub's work began on the island of Patmos! Furthermore, a Dr. Eiberg and his team found a specific gene, known as the **OCA2 gene,** which if altered would result in human beings without melanin in their hair, eyes, or skin color – a condition known as albinism. Hence, this OCA2 gene was targeted and manipulated by some force or event around 6,000+ years ago.

In a 2006 *New York Times* article is yet more proof of drastic alteration of genetic structure within this 6,000 year time frame. It reported researchers at the University of Chicago found "where genes *appear to have been reshaped by natural selection. Within the last 5,000 to 15,000 years." But incredibly, a Dr. Johnathan Pritchard estimates that the point in time when the genes of the Asian and European populations were altered was 6,600 years ago. The exact date in time the Messenger said that Mr. Yakub [Nubian like Christ], began his grafting process!

Western-Euro-Scientists, "Selected genes may underlie present-day differences in appearance but exactly **"how, when or why"** modern-day White-scientists will not say. However, in a human timeline of millions of years this recent genetic alteration is so drastic indeed suggests a motive or purpose-driven effort [like the Nubian], to create this incredible change.

All the above has as much truth to believe, as well a love for gold have its origin as humanity itself in Africa. Even until today, the wealthiest ever in history, was Africa's Black man **Mansa Musa.** Kings of Mali, Africa were referred to by title "Mansa." 1235 AD gave the Mali Empire access to the **"Trans-Saharan Trade Routes."** The "Trans-Sahara trade" required travel across the Sahara desert [was greenery, had foliage back-then] to reach Sub-Sahara **Nubia,** Africa.

From the North African coast. To Europe, the Levant (Israel) and **China.** While existing from prehistoric times, the peak of trade extended from the 8th until the 17th century. Black **Kemet** named Egypt by the Greek, called Nubians, and Nubian means **"Gold,"** like Mansa Musa these Africans were rich!

POWER COMES FROM LAW

We tell it like it is about evildoers, are corrupters onto the law of our God ... A special Notice: - Shows President Trump of 2025, a fascist autocrat, never speaks on raising **"the minimum-wage"** to live on, and not the, at present sacrificing to make ends meet. The minimum-wage at present is pitifully, only $7.25 an hour. This minimum-wage is pathetically $6.00 less than what it would have been in the 1950s! Why? Hum ... Must end. Understand, it takes talent to make money. Then rightly so, you learn how to keep it!

Read our examined, studied, contemplated, and highly researched factual *information, and other earlier editions such as: *"NUBIANS ORIGINATORS OF WORLD HISTORY,"* a "family heirloom" at only $24.99. Republicans are doing-away with democracy. Trump is a wanna-be dictator. He's proving it! Humane Republican politics remaining, is our concern for "you the people." Only with truth, honesty and common-sense. Stay strong and wise, having eyes in the back of your head ... Hum!

We here fight hard, because standing UNITED against discrimination is "anti-racism" **law** in Court! An old Nubian American saying [the author] said: "The blacker the berry the sweeter the juice! Give me a barrel of them black berries, cause, au, I'm jet-black!!!" To the Christian "God bless," and to the Islamic Nation, "As-Salaam Alaikum." All others peace, "So-long" ... The most worst of "**Nihilism**" in the **world** now at present, is in **SUDAN!** Nihilism (1: a viewpoint that traditional values and beliefs are unfounded and that existence is senseless and useless 2: ANARCHISM - nihilist. Is trying to erase the Black man from his land and history is the Rev. 2:9 Euro-Jew and White man's hidden and secret ideology. The Republican now coup boldly lie distracting truth; Nubian Americans must fight and win democracy here, overflows to **SUDAN!**

Devastating humanitarian crisis; <u>displaced</u> are **14 million** people, by "outsiders involvement, escalation and of a prolonged <u>civil war</u>" has <u>killed</u> over **150,000** in Sudan. Is more than **Ukraine** and the horrible inhumane crisis in **Gaza** put together! Seems like, White man's intention with Yakub' s left instructions they would rule for 6,000 years, boosted their aim; in "involvement history," is to distort by extending his time-frame on earth to rule. More or less his White man "Adam and Eve" so-called beginning is to conflict and dispute the 6,600 years his true creation; by Sudan's Nubian great scientist, **Yakub.**

Ashkenazi actually means 'north.' **Mizrahi** Jews lived east. **Sephardi** Jews lived 'west' and Ashkenazi lived north from their reference point that described "the Holy Land." In its infinite weirdness, decided in the early twentieth century that all Middle Easterners were supposedly White people! Why does the Black man always run into this dilemma in his depicted history and Hollywood movies, the White man try so hard to make the anyway, so-called Middle-East, and northeast Africa depicted White people! Knowing good and well they were all Black people the **Greek** way back in the beginning of their learning from African teachers the sciences, said, "Burnt faces" black from the sun. Also, back then in the beginning, a man was judged by his deeds and good standings, not by his skin color was just another man. Until the Middle-Ages the <u>bigoted</u> and <u>racist</u> White man changed all of that. However, we the people UNITED with the "**vote**" and "**law**" in the Court; will change all of that!!!

Converted Euro-Jews and White Christian Nationalist with a white-supremacy (hoax) belief ideology, is uncalled-for, having a fragile **ego** that envy, imitate, and copy. In jealousy; target with malicious racist-hate, towards Black, Brown, and Muslims. In "Racism" that is not good, "**Is against the Law**," that brings with it damage, injury and death. The pernicious darkness in America that contest any **Honesty**; permeates from a sorry and corrupt presidency at present, Trump, having no moral compass nor mental stability to rightly govern **the Peoples** nation, guardian of its **Law** and **Constitution** of the Land. He violates without "**Legal Authority**", to do!

However, Black Women's political **genius** is emphatically in support of her people, who built this world's strongest nation with red blood, like everyone else, sweat from mostly torturous hard labor, and tears from **death** and injustices, deserve at last, "**Honor and Respect**" we here give, helping also the good no matter how little in all of us of humanity, in these trying-times in America. Because, most Whites fear what goes around the evil they have caused around the world, will come around to them, we Black folks will **avoid**, with "**honest truth**" in this book; "**Let Us Make Man.**" Has left no history-stone deservedly unturned we, fair you well in peace!

****

Nubian Americans Identity Rise DNA Proof

Albert Fortney Jr.

TABLE OF CONTENTS

    Illustrations

1. Introduction – The Fortney Encyclical History Ed. Co. — 116
2. The Fortney Encyclical History Ed. Co. — 118
3. The Fortney Encyclical History Ed. Co. – "Theme Topic" — 120
4. The Fortney Encyclical History Ed. Co. – Research — 122
5. "To My Nubian Queen — 126
6. Illustrations
7. "Hidden Nubian Genius Rise" — 136
8. Affidavit of Nubian American: U.S.A. Census Info. — 139
9. Affidavit Nubian American Identity: Census Appendix — 144
10. Illustrations
11. Affidavit Nubian American Identity: Appendix Conclusion — 151
12. "We are Proven Nubian Americans" — 153
13. "Ancient Nubian Gold Economics Study" — 156
14. Illustrations
15. "Wooly-Hair Christ was a Black Nubian" — 168

**He ain't heavy
He's my brother**

Africa under full glacial conditions

Africa under full glacial conditions was North Africa before the White man dug-out the Suez Canal that wrongly dismantled geographically part of the African Continent, Africa rejected too. Because 250 miles offshore is larger than France; Island Madagascar still is the African Continent.

Egypt Sinai Peninsula

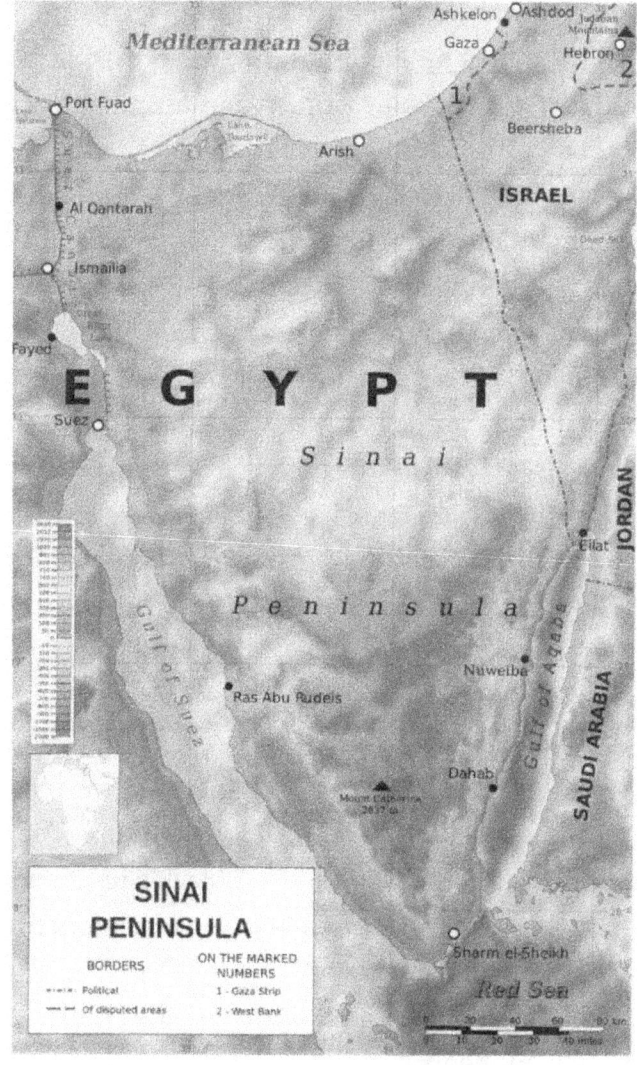

INTRODUCTION – The Fortney Encyclical History Ed. Co.

The Black Man's historian concern of his world history, demands the attention to his **kinky wooly-hair image** as the **"Nubian American identity."** Means a recognition **not** here, as <u>African</u> <u>Americans</u>. **No longer** the use of African American a **continent's** <u>title</u>; of a descriptive but not an **"identity"** usage for the importance in education, resource power, prehistory & ancient great achievements till today; and especially black businesses in America, with a **mark of distinction** that stands for **"NUBIAN."** Threw-out U.S. history, Nubian Americans have **blessed** America.

Cush (Kush), is the name of a once great ancient kingdom in **"Northeast Africa."** According to the Bible, Cush was the son of Ham a descendant to her neighbor, Ethiopia. By the Greeks, "Cushi" is a **HEBREW** term for a black person. As late as the 1940s and 50s, the racial identity of Nubians were and remained problematic for "white" scholars; even when bones of Kushite royalty were recovered from the "Reisner's excavations" and sent to specialists at the Museum of Harvard, they identified them as belonging to the "basic white stock of Egypt." White scholars left no doubt about their biases to dismiss the Nubian rule of Egypt's 25th Dynasty "black kings;" now recognized as the renaissance of Egyptian's great engineering, art, and culture. They soon figured-out how to appease wooly-haired black's resentment of being called colored, blacks and Negroes with a pacifying permissible, incorrect usage of African Americans.

Know this absolute wisdom, that the Nubian American of the African Continents past Biblical Cush Empire, is the unseen space "Alien" by the white man's History Channel, who's creative blackness is overlooked and seems unrecognizable to the 6,000 years old bias Caucasian. That there must be something else as smart as white but certainly not black; even though all the facts points to the contrary!!! Just like, not up-dating "schoolroom text," that the Egyptian Nubian great pyramid was a "nuclear power-plant," and not a royal burial ground. Was unrecognizable to explain without recent modern-day knowledge of nuclear "isotopes." The high intelligence, of prehistory black man scientists also created the blonde-hair blue eyed Aryan in 600 years on Patmos Island; with "graftation" of blacks to white that Islam in detail explains, what National Geographic's verified his first appearance 6,000 yrs. ago; he **omits** in his story of history. He'd rather depict from an **ape**, while whitewashing black <u>lands and history</u> as his…he can't about us <u>Nubians</u>. This time wherever the truth was lost, here's the **WHOLE** truth.

If they don't feel guilty or have no remorse over the <u>evil</u> they've done and **"<u>lying</u>"** on us then we, don't feel guilty on telling the truth about their **'birth'** and <u>evil</u> <u>deeds</u> that follow almost all of them. **<u>White</u> <u>nationalism</u> <u>racists</u>** are trying to <u>steal</u> "democracy of freedom" away from black and brown people, for the white privileged and **white supremacist**. Jan. 6, 2021 was a **death** day **'insurrection'** of the capital building, by **racist American terrorists**. Their objective is removal of the vote and blocking black and people of color from obtaining "resource power" under a <u>guise</u> of Christian conservative's supporting a **fascist** like leader **Trump** (Ashkenazi Jew), claiming it's justifiable for a <u>pure</u> "white America." You play by good rules, law and deed to move forward.

The Fortney Encyclical History Ed. Co.

"America's Best Kept Secret – Nubian Americans." History has not been recorded fairly of the wooly-hair black-man, but kind only for the white-man because "they" have written it in many instances a fiction (lie) they settled upon in agreeing. For 500 years, they have insultingly manipulated their image, story, and texts of so-called history to the majority population; black and brown people of the world. St. John 8: 44 – Ye are of *your* father the devil, and the lusts of your father ye will do. …a murderer… there is no truth in him…he is a liar and the father of it.

We're describing Euro-Caucasians and Semite white looking southwestern Asian Jew nomad converts to Judaism of the Black Hebrew religion. Rev. 2: 9 – I know thy works, and tribulation, and poverty, (but thou art rich) and *I know* the blasphemy of them…say they are Jews, and are not, but *are* the synagogue of Satan. Once ancient biblical Cush (Kush), is now called SUDAN; the largest country in Africa. Nubia (Sudan), is what the ancient Romans called it and in Africa.

In 1909, American Euro-Egyptologist George Reisner said that, Nubia was governed by "white" Libyans in Africa, mind you who supposedly created this black ancient civilization. Then later changed to a black governed people. The place where hieroglyphic writing was first discovered, where magnificent temples and mastery of pyramids were already built while Egypt was in its infancy didn't know existed as the original "cradle of the arts, sciences, and civilization," is kept from being depicted as **"black-skin"** text in the American school systems.

The devious of evil in Caucasian and Semite rule, created its made-up, false "cradle of civilization" area around the Tigris and Euphrates Rivers (once was **Africa**), in Iraq, 3,000 B.C. Mesopotamia. By-passed by omitting, the 5,000 B.C. Nubian established civilization, of a true **"wooly-hair"** black-man history. Why, is the rich history of Nubia overlooked for **"Nubian Americans"** rightful identity; wrongly called African American (as a "lost identity")?

Great black "Nubian Queens" were, Shanakdakhete, Tiye, Amani Rina, and Kandake Amanirenas, who skillfully defended her kingdom against "Caesar's Roman Empire" from conquering her homeland. And several wooly-hair "Nubian Kings" ruled Egypt's 25th Dynasty.

The new hydroelectric Kajabar Dam, located 250 miles south of the Egyptian-Sudanese border in Sudan, will cover with water dozens of their last remaining villages and inhumane, brazenly displacing tens of thousands of people, Nubians "protest." The Kajabar Dam will also flood ancient Nubian monuments, along with other antiquities dating to 5,000 years ago. "There are no Nubians in the dam area. There are only Arabic tribes. "Lied," they are not the original Nubians," says (paid) Al-Khatim Abdullah press adviser to Sudanese Embassy in Cairo, Egypt.

The government has not provided a relocation project, he says, because it still needs funding. However, risks to the great Nubian culture remain. Think about this enough to respond because Nubians will need all the help they can get. Rightly and adequately preserve, their outstanding first in creative traditions. The grand historian author, February 18, 2022 (Friday).

****

The Fortney Encyclical History Ed. Co. – "Theme Topic"

"America's next best kept secret – Nubian American's identity." **Identity Means Everything.** It's Northeast Africa's Nubia (Sudan's biblical Cush [Kush]), of ancient 5,000 BC – 500 AD geography of history to visit. Is a fact, the most important to view of ancient "wooly-haired black skin history," that represents the greatest people of today, is the "<u>Nubian American</u>."

Anti-black racists deem anything in an ancient black-man culture, or African black context is in their view doesn't have the meaning, it obviously have, to them is other than Africa. Nubians (Cushites), were excellent bow and arrow archers of war and were characterized largely as a militaristic people in the Hebrew Bible. Military engagement references to Cush (2 Chronicles 14:9-15; Isaiah 20:3-4; Jeremiah 46:9; Ezekiel 30:4-5, 38:5; Nahum 3:9). Isaiah 18:2 characterizes the Cushite people was **"feared near and far,"** and a mighty nation of conquering, **"supreme."**

Joel 2:25 God promises that He will restore all that was taken away in the years that the devil was tearing down the "church." Biblical Ethiopia (Nubia) is Genesis 10. God is reforming to bring restoration of the original faith and away from European "tradition" and "theology."

Nubian military reputation was consistent in ancient Egypt and had spread throughout the ancient Near East. However, far from skin-color hate we see in the physical characteristics racist concerns today, the Ancient Cushite (Nubian), Egyptians, Assyrians, and Greeks had NO negative racist <u>black</u> <u>nor</u> <u>white</u> skin-color racialized view of identity. **Identity Knows History!!!**

Amos 9:7, presents an almost sameness between black wooly-hair Israelites and Cushites: Are you not like the Cushites to me, O Israel, declares our Lord, Yahweh, Christ. But Rabbinate (Ashkenazi of Genesis 10:3) provides their explanation: "Israel's Christ is no more than his own uncivilized, and despised black race of Ethiopians"...and the fact that wooly-hair "slaves" were so often made of them added to despising them. In the 15th century AD, Gentiles created racism.

Also the beliefs of today's modern influence, and unwarranted assumptions always remind us, are the ancient Cushites until today's wooly-hair Nubian Americans, once "despised" black slaves. This trajectory was from biblical observation into the 20th century till today, explicit anti-black racist sentiments are directly to Nubian Americans (ex-Negros, ex-African Americans).

Ancient Nubian identity by black and brown people, was also by their wooly afro-textured kinky hair. Cornrow and braided hairstyles, were historically worn to signify marital status, age, religion, wealth and rank was an important sacred spiritual symbol that was proudly worn.

In Amos 9:7, Israel is compared in sameness to Cush because both nations will experience Yahweh's (Jesus Christ) judgment and salvation. The Amos passage teaches us that ancient identities are specified ethnically, nationally, tribal, in **stone** or geographically because it is too convenient for interpreters to put or read "their own values" into biblical text. A man, is supposedly to be the symbol of strength, **truth**. The Nubian American (descendant of Cushites), is said more, **"righteous by nature."**

****

The Fortney Encyclical History Ed. Co. - Research

Our company represents, **"We the People,"** seekers of truth. Truth are Nubian American's experiences for the best interest, and their light for the world that will set you free; is like food with the bodies mechanism, that creates energy for the body to function and perform. **"The Truth Is The Light."** Anything else is a so-called, alternate-truth (fiction, a lie, untrue, incorrect, false and just plain wrong). This so-called truth (lies), is why black people are despised and hated to death by racist and white nationalist changing of black history as they choose…

Asks the question, why are all King James Version biblical characters depicted Caucasians? Another thing, America is teaching its children an alternate-truth in education that supposedly is properly teaching students, how to think correctly and grow, to function and perform in life. They have actually applied this alternate-truth in "history."

Whether they realize it or not, they're subconsciously and indirectly teaching hate to despise black people; by leaving out the black man's great cultural accomplishments in Africa's past and first civilization; instead of constant expounding on servitude and demeaning **slavery;** that they believe is good enough and deserving of black people. Black lives does matter and those against it, must stand accountable for their guilt, of their backwards evil actions and atrocities.

The atrocities we deem responsible against black people's progression also are:
1. Unseen targeting of domestic sanctions by crippling business resources that causes unemployment
2. Manipulate unjust and unbalanced law and order equality against black and brown peoples

3. Restrict black man's cultural "knowledge of self," with abuse of power depicting religion with a white-supremacy "misleading history narrative," in educational institutions and entertainment medias
4. Institute a much poorer-black educational system, to hinder, the invaluable role to children's education make
5. Implement poisonous health conditions, by living in locations of placement, close to industrial toxins

    All these sufferings are preventable by the constitution. Black and brown people can't stand for none of this and must echo loud our thoughts. It's said amongst all black people, that we have to be "twice as good to get ahead;" to make-up for obstacles whites will put in your way they couldn't do, if the other way around. However, we are succeeding, but not fast enough with systemic racist roadblocks. America must stop, rationalizing away its responsibility to take action for we the people starts now, immediately today, and not the "<u>stuff</u>-<u>off</u>" with soon or tomorrow. We don't have to love but we must **"respect each other"** in order to **co-exist** should be a common understanding but taught **"a priority"** with the first amendment protecting freedom of speech.

    A sixth grade student in Florida told a substitute teacher he wouldn't stand for the pledge because he believed the American flag symbolized discrimination against blacks. He was arrested because he started a disturbance police claimed. Atheistic or religious freedom groups tried to eliminate the phrase "under God" from the pledge. The first amendment shouldn't protect blasphemous and <u>fraudulent depicted text</u>, of black-man's original cultural heritage history as a fictional (lie) white-man's creation that does extreme harm to the "original belief." If so, would it not represent **"<u>double-jeopardy</u>,"** to permit a <u>white-supremacy-exception</u> to the rules of the first amendment rights; to rewrite with pictured deceptive white history as his own, of black history???

Racism was created in Europe during the 15th century Middle Ages to deceive, that gave way to doing harm, hurt and despising of Africa's black man, especially it's Sudan (Nubia) ancient Cush history (Nubian American ex-Negro) world-wide. It seems, English biblical scholars (King James Version) try to keep Cushites other than a reference to Mesopotamia and only to identify to lands south of Egypt. It was their planning to wrongly justify a so-called "garden of Eden" all theirs "cradle of civilization in Mesopotamia" opposed to the true cradle of civilization south of Egypt in Nubia (Ethiopia), and an Israel Semite now, was once a **wooly-hair** ancient Nubian land. Parts of **Arabia** was once a part or region of **Africa,** and most certainly **Israel** (major land of Levant) was before the white-man carved-out the Suez Canal and deviously claimed (with poor excuses) it separated, Israel from the great black-man's **"Africa Continent."**

In early ancient times, skin-color wasn't a relevant issue or factor in identifying a people was rare, like in the life time of Christ the wooly-hair, black-skin color liberator. (Rev. 1:14-15 KJV) His head and *his* hairs *were* white like wool, as white as snow; and his eyes *were* as a flame of fire; 15 And his feet like unto fine brass, as if they burned in a furnace; and his voice as the sound of many waters.

Skin color back then was like hair color today, of seeing it but not really mentioning it. However, there really are no white people in the Holy Bible. Abraham, Moses, King Solomon, Deborah, Sheba, David, Elijah, Jezebel, Daniel, Jesus, Peter, Paul or Lydia and even the church **Rome** were not white; because whiteness hadn't existed yet, was thought of as **"tribes"** or **"nations"** Greek for nation is "ethnos" (ethnic). Some historical roots were cultural overlaps. Racism, was a baseless theory of putting white people at the top of the scale, red and yellow in between and black people at the very bottom.

Historically, white U.S.A. historian text teaches that their keen, they think, to up-play physical characteristics with Caucasian figures in the Bible, to manifest superiority of white spirituality. **"<u>Satan</u>,"** however being the prince of darkness is represented as a horned, winged black-man like figure to <u>despise</u> and <u>hate</u> is a white-man's <u>manufactured</u> image. To see a <u>devil</u> and his followers in life like movies would seem terrifying for an audience but an exhilarating experience for white nationalist, KKK terrorists or white supremacy racists.

The History Channel's **"<u>The</u> <u>Bible</u>"** mini-series did just that, with Moroccan actor Mohamen Medi Ouazanni (convenient to mar with envy, a President Obama look-alike), played the part of **Satan**. Dr. Martin Luther King Jr., emphasized that the color of one's skin doesn't determine the content of one's character. His statement attacked, the language and negative image of Nubian Americans men, women, and children that associated them to "<u>darkness with demonic evil</u>," and "whiteness with good." Across medieval Europe, they described <u>Satan</u> as dark or black.

The "<u>dark</u> <u>arts</u>," were known of <u>witches</u> in early colonial America. <u>Satan</u> did not only come in blackness or a red-devil, he could take any number of forms he needed. This had to have paved the way collectively for Caucasian and Semite children to grow up subconsciously if not direct <u>attitudes</u> with <u>hate</u> for the black-man; but gives no-excuse as he learned or instinctively knew, from his fabricated history that, he knows better than that!!!

<u>Racist</u> sufferings are preventable. We the people must not stand for none of this with action. We must echo loud our thoughts or indifference may to some other than black or brown, you're **"next."** War is <u>Satan</u>, **God help Ukraine...**

"To My Nubian Queen"

To a most *deserving lady* perhaps one day her speech, through a microphone on stage that represents *"perseverance"* makes you *"rightfully known,"* might go a little something like this:

The *"Fortney Encyclical History Ed. Co."* drums bellows their beat, loud across the U.S., with our deep concern to **"educate."** But keeping humility in mind with the **facts,** of major events and achievements. Many times hidden and standing in the back of the line from history; such as the "distinct wooly-hair trait" of **Nubian American's** (so-called ex-negroes). The **Sudan's** great and glorious ancient history still stands, also a great part of us being here is, **we the people.**

Just as if yes, there's a "secret cold-war" going on against us who are striving to only do good and not informed is a deadly wrong. Has the markings of old evil Satan and his diligent servant devils, against us same old but "more-righteous" **"wooly-hair"** people created in "God's image."

There is too much unnecessary things going-on that lack a common-decency, respect, and empathy towards those of color with evil racism. Being **Caucasian** or **Semite-Jew,** you wouldn't put on yourself. You have shown an increase in discrimination even during humanitarian crisis globally. You cry of "democracy," yet you are not the one swimming in those same dangerously turmoil waters, nor are you racked across hot coals of whitewashed racism. Is your hypocrisy, you continuously subject us Nubian American's... Forgiveness is costly and never is it forgotten.

Our prestigious history books for adults and the children's book of black history is astounding. Our books the Fortney Encyclical History Ed. Co. carry, are shining examples almost (so to speak) bursting at their seams with enlightenment, deserving to all people of different nationalities to service, **we the people!** Don't hesitate, "learn the sacred truth from <u>slavery</u> <u>to</u> <u>racism</u> of all time we are living in." And we also have concern for the <u>sad</u> people incarcerated, society has written off, are all God's children in His sight, in dire need of our book's learning that will help them.

Nubian American's, the **Nubian,** is a Godly people's history. The hair like lamb's wool Nubian civilization flourished in **Sudan** over 5,000 years ago **Africa,** was well before the birth of **Egypt.** The time spam may be off at least 10 to 12,000 years old, instead of the great pyramid's age being 2500 to 3000 years old by mainstream scientist's inaccuracy. It's known, the great pyramid and the Sphinx were built by them before the great flood, during the ice-age about 12,000 years ago. Nubians were great warriors and rulers of Egypt's 25th Dynasty. The "Turin Papyrus Map" is one of the oldest (1,600 BC) maps known, is of a "gold" mine in Nubia. Then why was Africa's great Nubian civilization completely bye-passed in American taught schoolhouse learning??

The white man's world history is a whitewashed (lie), favored to others (Semite-Jews) about us (Nubians), well before him the Caucasian was created 6,600 years ago, in small comparison. Africa's **pre-history** of black-skin Egyptians were original Nubian descendants, and not today's light-skin ad-mixtures of southwestern Asians, Semite Arabs, or Semite Euro-Jews <u>despising</u> us. Nubians, **creators** of engineering, math, law, the sciences, and religion before Egypt's honorable mentions, after us inspiring Nubians.

What is the real reason or why am I so <u>despised</u> and so <u>hated</u> like so-called jungle <u>savages</u>; as to keep <u>hidden</u> and <u>steal</u> my "true identity" locked away with my "great cultural heritage" from me in <u>slavery</u>; as being a **"Nubian American,"** and not colored or Negro and always only the "N" word nigger (at a black lynching) to <u>racist</u> whites, anything but Nubian American's "rightfully so?" Because the world's foremost astonishing great collection, of Nubian antiquities are at the **Boston Museum of Fine Arts (MFA)** in the 1980's however, bias projections led to racist convictions that considered Sub-Saharan Sudan's Nubia of Africa, a barbarized shadow of Egypt by European virtue of too much "Negro" infusion.

White America wants to accentuate Eurocentric reality even when it comes to all white biblical characters you view in a pictorial bible, makes no sense to truth, which represents a racist view towards ancient black kingdoms, cultures and nations till today must end. A rarity, but some wooly-hair Nubians have blue around the pupil of their eyes. And some of his Ethiopian ancestry neighbor's hair, is straight are facts of black Africa's genetics not explained in mainstream science.

What is white racism against a dark white? Here's a brief view, of a confusing understanding of "whites" racism, besides anti-Semite and anti-Nubian Americans. During the mid-19th to mid-20th century, race scientists and most anthropologists classified the European people and their descendants, "light whites" of Northern Europe with the "dark white" of the Mediterranean **"Slaves"** (the first slaves of history), were referred to as subhuman, and Eastern European countries such as Poland, Ukraine and the USSR (Russian) etc. was do, to the racial inferiority of their inhabitants was, to evil-rule doings.

Germany and Fascist **Italy** both had the same view, to falsely justify their colonial ambitions in Eastern Europe on racist anti-Slavic grounds were also not alone in this view. **Racism**, is the rawest and worst of devious evils to all races of peoples of the world that was prophesized and recorded by biblical historian scholars of ancient Sudan Cushite (**Nubians**). The Nazi, categorized the world's black and brown human races as "not human" and so evil (the Euro-Jews) as to deserve extermination; World War II's extreme of racism's **genocide**, goes against **"God's Law."**

Everyone should know, that humans did NOT evolve from

animals and animals have "fur" not **"hair,"** and if you remove the fur from monkey or ape (the unbelievable Darwin theory) their skin is pale white; so where does that leave the black man, certainly not coming from the white man. Clearly then, the wooly like, knotty (chiseled balls of hair knots for beards & hair in stone), or kinky hair is his **"proof"** that's so important. The **Nubians** were the "original humans" (made in **God's image** and known, more "righteous in nature" and with empathy) that asks the question (another issue) who was talking to whom when in the bible it said, **"Let us make man?"**

Nubian is able to create black, brown, red, yellow and white. While a white man and another Caucasian creates only Caucasian, is a fact of uncontestable truth. Whether there was a **natural selection** in migration of tribes that became different skin-colors, by black and brown progression of genetic mating or either the **grafting** theory of **Yakub;** who brought about the white race is now accepted his first appearance anywhere was 6,600 years ago.

The word Caucasian is actually a 19th century anthropological idea. It was based around a false conception that the origin of the human species was in the **Caucasus Mountains...** "Caucasians" is a white supremacist, racist ideology. Scientist found that the earliest humans didn't come from the Caucasus but from Sudan **Africa,** in modern day **Ethiopia** (Eden). Race is not supported by science. All peoples are of one species (Human). Humans are 99.9% identical in genetic make-up.

"Jesus Christ Acknowledged Being Nubian:" Though we already learned previously that there's so many times Ethiopia is represented and stood for the Biblical translation **Cush/Nubia,** and even the English King James version translate "Ethiopia for Cush," in Genesis 2:13. Black **"Moses"** married a **Cushite** woman (Numbers 12:1). And here is where, during the millennial rein of **Christ, Jesus** will receive honor from **Cush/Ethiopia:** "From beyond the rivers of

Cush my worshipers, my scattered people, will bring me offerings" (Zephaniah 3:10). Most certainly should be a great **"Biblical Sunday School Lesson"** around the whole-wide world to children.

True history depiction for elementary and high schooling learning that "teaches students how to think," should include a curriculum of the Sub-Saharan Africa, to Egypt and the Mediterranean civilizations as **"Nubian Study."** Giving all children a "same" chance to succeed. We're the renowned **Nubian Americans** of <u>ex</u>-<u>slaves</u>; whose ancestors contributed great accomplishments, advances to civilization itself that some are **marvels** modern man mysteries today can't solve such as the architect of the great, over 12,000 yrs. old **Pyramid** and **Sphinx** of Giza, Egypt. We built America with our blood, sweat and tears. It's a history that should be recognized in all institutions of learning around the world, because anything else would be **"uncivilized."**

The Euro-white man is trying to say he's a part of Mesopotamians, who are typically by him considered the very first urban (city) civilization along with the Sumerians in the world is fiction. It is a made-up and manufactured lie to eliminate, avoid telling or to get around by causing an Africa's black man's history of "<u>confusion</u>," to how he (whites) were **created;** when in the Bible blacks saying to other blacks said, **"Let us make man."** The white man is trying to fit himself in his history, as Caucasian "creating civilization." How dumb-founded he must feel saying he came from an <u>ape</u>, when he was a **Nubian/Egyptian** creation world's first civilization.

Fossil remains say the first human was the 2 million years ago Africa's black man, who supposedly appeared as modern-day man 200,000 was in Sub-Saharan Nubia/Ethiopia; and not a Euro-manufactured "cradle of civilization" in Mesopotamia's **Levant** (Israel, Iraq, Syria or Turkey etc.) called modern-day Anatolia. Despite humans living there longer than anywhere else, the **Sub-**

Saharan African built advanced civilizations are systematically denied and downplayed is because they are the hidden identity by whites, of the Nubian American's purposely and incorrectly called African Americans to try and keep a peoples great potentials ignorant of **"knowledge of self,"** that "cripples" a people's progress not knowing their strength to adequately progress, or not aware of their sense of power they possess to advance forward. **If you don't know who you are, then how the hell you know where you're going???**

Egyptians and the Great White Race Map

James Henry Breasted (1865-1935), was an American archaeologist who was regarded as one of the world's foremost authorities on the archaeology and history of Egypt and the Near East, which are collectively referred to as "the Orient." Breasted's views on the creation of Egyptian civilization by a "white race were also shared by one of his contemporaries, George Reisner. In 1916 Breasted stated Egyptians were a "brown-skinned race" and in 1935 he reversed himself and now said they were off the "Great White Race." Reisner claimed Nubia was originally governed by a dynasty of "white" Libyans, and all black dynasties were but extensions of them. Bruce Williams, an archaeological specialist of Nubian culture with the Oriental Institute decried the role racist ideologies played in distorting ancient Nile Valley history.

The Ancient Connection of Northeast Africa

This map gives the ancient connection of continental Africa to the neighboring northeastern land mass. Students, black folks and unknowing Americans have been led to believe by Western historians that Havilah (Arabia), Ethiopia, and Assyria (Mesopotamia), Persia, and Syria were separate and disconnected in their historical and geographical context, however, during biblical times they were very much connected. Since the river Niel flowed from southern Ethiopia and emptied into the Great Sea (Mediterranean) people migrated from lower Africa and journeyed to Northeast Africa (Canaan, Palestine) or today's Israel. There was no body of water to separate the two. The Suez Canal wasn't dug until the 19th century. And during War II war correspondents began to refer to North Africa and Northeast Africa as the "Middle East." The term "Middle East" disrespected by white required no need mention of Africa hence, avoid giving black recognition!

The Crucifixion

Moses the Law Giver

"Hidden Nubian Genius Rise"

The affluent ancient Nubian Empire is a vital subject of world history that was a "hidden" world history. Hidden as if forbidden beware… to always be by-passed in the schoolroom, by evil creators of "almost all untrustworthy white Christ believers." That in their evil rituals and occultism, are practiced, deceitful tactics, devious schemes and depictions of lies against truth, of the Black man; from a special continent rich in great mineral wealth, and the birth place of justice, spirituality, and intellect seems God intended an always Black man's land, "Africa."

The envies of greedy White men, are trying to claim the whole Northern part of Africa, from east to west depicted in Egyptian dress as building the great pyramid for example. The great Nubian Ethiopian blood-line Sub-Sahara, Sudan ancestor, was the world's first civilization; as God of good or the Devil with his lies know; was before either made-up Mediterrean first birth of civilization of Whites, Semite – Arab or Jew or mixing to a fiction depicted "Garden of Eden."

Then having to accept, the white skin-color assassination of the proven Black man Christ nailed and dying on the cross is parallel to like Nubian American's pain of not accepting but "forced," to view the stolen false image everywhere so much so, that the original black Christ should turn over in his grave from the insult. But is more like the double cross of Arabs to Euro-Jew owners of the slave market, had slaves delivered by Portuguese slave ship runners; causing over 100 million to their death, (over twice the population of the largest European country of Ukraine at 44 million), at the bottom of the Atlantic Ocean from abhorrent conditions aboard ship; now all the time blacks forced to seeing white police killings of unarmed, innocent black & brown men, women and children in America harms us, in the "land of the free & justice for all."

White-Jews to the contrary, hasn't suffered from racist pain since 1945 WWII, until now but why in Ukraine? Seems like some kind of balance; in a black & white "poetic justice of nature," but God bless them, in answering the question. And the dire need for Nubian American targets, must have "Victim-Laws" against police brutality "hate crimes" & "racist killings" in America.

In all of history seriousness, how's the white man going to write black man history but in all favor to himself? The answer is simple, they lied! However, the black man is rejecting the white man's perspective writing black man's history he's serving the black man, about the black man. The racist challenge emboldens us to do twice as better our job for intensely honest black man history. We have a lot to get into. We get our objective done focused on our Nubian history that must be known and getting it published for all societies to learn of their accomplishments if any. Starting from pre-history, is not hoping to be a society but is recognized, as the black essence that began in Ethiopia.

It's not as if seeming the impossible was done by blacks, but the black man did do what is thought impossible and was the first; moving unimaginable colossal carved stones with the lost genius of black technology of **"Levitation;"** is a feared feat of power, that scares the white man unable to achieve today what blacks did, so he "fantasizes a fictional lie" it must was done by some outer-space "aliens," only to discredit the Nubian's "wooly-haired genius and truth."

If anything, the alien here is the first appearance of the different white man minority on earth; and not the other way around, to the majority of people overwhelmingly with the miraculous magic performing **"Melanin,"** with a much higher count in black and brown peoples. Creates from the sun's rays into what the architect genius was, the Nubian's "gift" to his descendant neighbor, are "the great pyramids" of Giza to his Egyptian black brothers and sisters. The story of pre-history "flight" (another hidden event) and "ancient electric dry-cell batteries" discovered in "old" **Africa,** is for a later discussion. Grandmother (Bi-Ma born the month of April 1898) use to say, "Nothing is new under the sun." 'Tis true…'tis so true. He hides history, wanting us "inert" of doing our unimaginable plus, full potential to do!!!

AFFIDAVIT OF NUBIAN AMERICAN: U.S.A. Census Info.

Any question of legal argument that may arise of black-people's **"hair like lamb's wool"** confirmation of our ancestral identity as part of **we the people,** asks with all due respect recognized as **Nubian American** "identity" of a **country** (not new but to the census), and no longer as Colored, Negro or the African American "title" of a **continent** whites are also "born."

But we are a "wooly-hair" recognizable blood-line tribal **Nubian Americans,** Euro-American historians of society hide, what must change and corrected in identity schooling. They suppress from the public mass media, what even **"DNA"** technology supports. According to the Y-DNA analysis of 2008, shows that **44%** of Nubians carry haplogroup J, followed by **24%** with haplogroup E11b (also known as **E-M215**). The haplogroup J branch J-M267, is carried by Nubians is found in high ratios in North Africa, the Horn of Africa, Yemen, and Assyrians.

On the mitochondrial DNA maternal (motherly) linage **30.8** of Nubians have the **L3** mt-haplogroup, which originated in **Northeastern Africa.** Second in order, **20.6%** of Nubians have the mt-haplogroup L0a close to the "Mitochondrial Eve," significant in **South Africa, Mozambique. 10.3%** of Nubians have the **L2** clade of mt-haplogroup L, originated in **East Africa,** migrated to **West Africa,** strong in **Senegal (43-54%).** In conclusion, they are confusingly basic **Afro-Nubian** people, having part **Niger-Congo** people and part **Bantu** people; dominate **wooly hair** – 4a to 4c ='s, exclusive to blacks of African ancestry, ex-slave **"Nubian Americans."**

They were not created yet, to tell us who we was, and so they omitted us ancient Nubians from his depicted history. We were never **conquered,** with more defining proof we wrote of us, **"chiseled in stone pre-history."** There's no question of worth in the

Sudan Sub-Saharan, to the future who's now in America; of our great **achievements,** and **ruled** Egypt in her **peak** of great history.

When most so-called African Americans take a DNA test it show they are related to ancient Nubians. Now, even DNA shows that many so-called African Americans are descendants of **"Ancient Nubians"** that out of racism's too many "so-called educated," miss-educated and uneducated purposely ignore this fact. Because no one has ever found proof of the biblical Exodus until the study of the Ancient **Cushite,** "Nubians." The Holy Bible the "Black" man wrote and Black Jewish Hebrew calls Ancient Nubia **"Goshen,"** to which is strenuously problematic for "White" groups considering themselves religiously or racially superior.

Nubian's history is well known to the white man in the western hemisphere, who's black man term we come from "Kings and Queens" represent the black man, his women and children's **"Nubian Queen"** (a flattering term) describe black people, in a racist hemisphere. However today, a small section of Africa's Nubians are somewhat an Arabized people but basically not a major shift since the Arab migrations into North Africa just as in Egypt.

The genetics of the Abusir el-Meleq community that did not undergo any major shifts during the **1,300-year timespan** studied, and group leader at the Max Planck Institute Krause said, "A lot of people assumed foreign invaders brought genetic ancestry into the region. People thought through time, Egypt would become more European but we see just the **exact opposite.**" Modern Egyptians were found to **inherit 8%** more ancestry from **African** ancestors than the mummies studied. Increased long distanced commerce with the **Meroe** Nubian metropolis of the "gold trade" and the trans-Saharan slave trade are potential reasons why.

Half of the sub-Saharan mtDNA sequences in the database are common haplotypes that are shared among ethnic groups from multiple regions of sub-Saharan Africa. Fewer than 10% of so-called

African American mtDNA matched mtDNA sequences from a single African region. Suggests that, one in nine so-called African Americans may be able to trace their mtDNA to a particular region in Africa. However, so-called African Americans mtDNA are identical to African haplotypes found in multiple ethnic groups throughout sub-Saharan Africa you can't use only mtDNA sequence information to determine a single group was the maternal ancestor.

Mitochondrial DNA tests trace people's matrilineal (mother-line) ancestry through their mitochondria, which any two people will have an identical mitochondrial DNA sequence if they are related by an unbroken maternal line. How far back can mitochondrial DNA be traced? We can trace the mtDNA back to a woman from about **150,000 to 200,000 years ago,** that everyone on the planet is related to. And the Y chromosome to a man we're all related to from **60,000** or so years ago. Scientists have named them **Mitochondrial Eve & Y Adam,** in 5/18/2012.

The percentage of human diversity between humans is about **"0.1 percent."** What we think of as "races" are socially assigned or better yet, white man sets of characteristics that change depending on context. Is race a social construct or biological? In the biological and social sciences, the consensus is very clear in history: race is a **social construct** (a white man's creation such as <u>white supremacy racism</u>), and not a meaningful mankind biological **attribute.**

In **anthropological** genetics, mtDNA is useful to trace geographic distribution of genetic variation, for the investigation of expansions, migrations and other pattern of gene flow. Also, mtDNA is widely applicable in **"forensic science."** That is a powerful implement, to identify human remains that has a purposeful use that really matters.

To determine an individual's race, people may use one or more ancestry or biological bases or **physical characterizes** (most likely) and cultural bases, such as ideology and language. Race can't be found in our genes but biological ancestry is **real** that differs in race. The geographic isolation, and three great human races in the last 5,000 to 7,000 years that split our species are: **Africans** (once so-called <u>racist</u> Negroid), **Caucasoid** (or Europeans) and **Mongoloid** (or Asians).

What percentage Sub-Saharan DNA is shared ancestry DNA with so-called African Americans, proven are actually Nubian Americans? Answer is a walloping **14%!!!** Are all people descendants of Black people? The facts support a correct **"yes,"** and not any theory or conjecture by the experts in the area of learning; that causes a great deal of discomfort to those believing in "<u>White Supremacy</u> Fraud" of any kind. Because there's only "one race," the human race **"One Specie."** **God bless all Americans** especially at her bottom, poor **Nubian Americans.** This validates & answers a Nubian American census question, that's a "national confirmation."

Incidentally before we go, if you was wondering what **Goshen** meant, it's a region of ancient Egypt, east of the Nile delta; granted to Jacob and his Black **Israelite** descendants by the king of Egypt and inhabited by them until the Exodus (Genesis 45:10) for generations of children a place of comfort and plenty. The original Black Hebrew settlement located along the fringe where the delta farmland meets the eastern desert.

In Biblical names **Goshen** is: **"Approaching, drawing near"** just as the risen acceptance **soon,** of the Nubian American view of reality history that was **"<u>Hidden</u>"** to make this country a White nation alone; separated between two great oceans to experiment with freedoms aside (out of the way) from God to have complete control of others. Perhaps, America is todays "big-bro" **Israel.**

In human genetics, the White (Caucasian) race is derived from haplogroup R is a Y-chromosome DNA haplogroup, subgroup of haplogroup P, defined by the M207 mutation. The "American Dream," expressed as happiness through material wealth, was never intended for Nubian Americans. We reject <u>historical brainwashing</u> wherein white society teaches <u>falsely</u> that Nubian Americans were <u>savages</u> who were civilized through <u>slavery</u> and accomplishments that were Nubians instead were white. This <u>falsity</u> of white history originated and ends with their desire to hide their true nature on a fabricated concept that has become **dangerously** delusional.

America is an example of democracy achieved for whites only, even after **Nubian American <u>slaves</u>** built it. Absolute power sets the stage for absolute <u>evil</u>. Whiteness has set the standard in America that's soon in changing as a fact, **"nothing remains the same."** Nubian Americans will rise again, aspire to "prominence & power" as **Biblical scriptures foreseen with prophesy…** And above everything else, it is our **job** and **duty,** at the *Fortney Encyclical History Ed. Co.* to *elevate* and *assent* the *Nubian American cause;* with these lessons of the *real story* implicitly of *facts,* with God's truth in *evidence* and let it fall where it may; to *thwart* other's <u>misleading **depicted** evilness in history</u> against God's *true image* **"The Black Man,"** (without instituting <u>black</u> <u>racism</u> of any kind), only with knowledge, understanding and it's *wisdom to all.*

AFFIDAVIT NUBIAN AMERICAN IDENTITY: Census Appendix

"Labels & Titles" were intentionally given just to give us a demeaning status, of a once enslaved people as property. Black American's are not generationally less human beings. Our heritage ties us to identify, as **Nubian American.** Describes a <u>kinky wooly-haired</u> Black person's ethnicity and race, from other parts of the world other than Africa. For example, a person may identify as a Black African and some with straight hair, like Asian Blacks of India's people with black-skin. However, the kinky wooly-hair declaration distinguishes between the two (once made fun of in White man's Jim Crow era), however **"Hair-Power $$$"** is now very important.

"Diversity" is dissolving race into **"identity."** Euro-America was fully aware, but hid from us in their education of learning, of our **Africa Nubia's** kinky wooly-hair identity in education; just as they used whitewashing Cleopatra in Black Egypt's Africa, and Black history they worked so hard to cover-up with extreme measures. Their deception was, try making her pure white wearing "Klan" suites as historian scholars, with "white privilege supremacy" a cause.

What Cleopatra fought hard to **preserve** was Egypt is Black Africa, like wooly-hair Blacks here as **Nubian Americans.** At the least, if an add-mixture of 30% to even 50% outside Egyptian but by white people's one-drop own standards, makes you a Black human being. Allowing false depicted history, has a rippling effect of harming. To exclude <u>Nubian American</u> identity is to exclude Cleopatra being black, the Bible explaining the black Jesus Christ, of Europe and South American's Black Madonna's Christ, and all of black history as **falsely** "white."

White man's creation of lying with racism, **controls** indigent blacks to an extent "life and death" indirectly saying, he's the creator of civilization with alien workers such as slaves or now space beings other than earth! Racist historian belief says, if **Nubia History** is allowed, it refutes, goes against and exposes all Euro-U.S.A. school-house histories that were lies, with whitewashed claims of all **North Africa** to **Israel.** And so, **identifying** the <u>Nubian American</u> had to be omitted in white man's world history. However, endeavors of today's <u>Nubian American</u> has risen to America's surface, for confirmation census. Thank you.

Our Precious Children

Money goes for cheap labor, jobs going overseas. Our black children shouldn't grow-up in despair, needing a partner collision to 'do for self,' to own our own economic culture. Things are bad but in 'unity' there is always strength.

3,000 Years Old Helicopter, Submarine ETC.

ABU SIMBEL TEMPLES complex: A miracle carved in the mountains that date back to Ramses II, 13th century BC are in **Nubia**, and wrongly depicted many times in history as in Egypt is our books cover. However, a **3,000 years old helicopter, submarine** etc. (above) is above an entrance of the Egyptian **Temple of Seti I.**

The Sacred Black Madonna

The sacred Black Madonna of Jasna Gora according to traditional history, was painted by the Gospel Maker Luke. It is said Luke drew 'two' Madonnas, and that one of these is in Czestochowa. We in America do not know, that when the Polish Pope each time he returns to Poland visits the shrine there, of the Virgin of Czestochowa or The Black Madonna, the first virgin and Black Child, wo later evolved into Mary and Jesus, before becoming WHITE with the help of Michelangelo, between 1508 and 1512 at the commission of Pope Julius II who was a "warrior pope" who in an aggressive campaign for political control to unite and empower Italy under the leadership of the church. A copy of the "Translario tabulae" dating from 1474 is kept in me archives of the monastery Jasna Gora. According to scholarly version, the picture was originally a Black Byzantine icon of the "Hodegerria," "she who shows the way," from between the 6th and the 9th century. Judaism rejects that Jesus was the awaited Messiah, prophecies in the Tanakh. In Islam, Jesus (Arabic translation is Isa) is considered an important prophet of God, of a virgin birth, worker of miracles. Islam and the Baha'l faith, title "Messiah" for Jesus.

Akebu-Lan means "Mother of Mankind" Map

Akebu-Lan is the oldest and means "Mother of Mankind" or "Garden of Eden," was used by the Moors, Nubians, Numidians, Khart-Haddans (Carthagenians), and the name Africa was given to this continent by the Romans. In 1,675 B.C. neither the name Jew nor Negro existed. The term Negro was given to the Blacks as they left Africa for slave ships 1,500 A.D. when the name "Negroland" was used. This term coined by the Portuguese meant "black." This term saved the slave traders having to identify each slave whether he was a Cushite, Ethiopian, or a Abyssinian, sometimes called in the bible. England and Portugal knew well these peoples whom they captured and chained, many times helped by ambitious Arabs, were the first ones to carry and establish Christianity and Judaism in Africa, northeast Africa, and Europe. Western bias whites have so foiled, baffled, defeated and blocked the history of the 'Black Race' so extensively, that it takes great study and research to 'unravel' his maze of myths, pictorial lies and confusion.

The Ancient Connection of Northeast Africa

This map gives the ancient connection of continental Africa to the neighboring northeastern land mass. Students, black folks and unknowing Americans have been led to believe by Western historians that Havilah (Arabia), Ethiopia, and Assyria (Mesopotamia), Persia, and Syria were separate and disconnected in their historical and geographical context, however, during biblical times they were very much connected. Since the river Niel flowed from southern Ethiopia and emptied into the Great Sea (Mediterranean) people migrated from lower Africa and journeyed to Northeast Africa (Canaan, Palestine) or today's Israel. There was no body of water to separate the two. The Suez Canal wasn't dug until the 19th century. And during War II war correspondents began to refer to North Africa and Northeast Africa as the "Middle East." The term "Middle East" disrespected by white required no need mention of Africa hence, avoid giving black recognition!

AFFIDAVIT NUBIAN AMERICAN IDENTITY: Appendix Conclusion

It is what it is but why, was the back-bone nation's fundamental foundation of great Africa's **pre-history;** *"world's first statue monuments"* carved in *mountainous stone* as evidence and in fact, was a Sudan Nubian **Nubia's** civilization whose rulers built **cities** isn't taught to us? Learnt was "Egypt & Mesapotamia" they did a job-on whitewashing; but dared-tamper in Nubia, Africa's, **"The Nubian Gateway"** where rich deposits of **gold,** ivory, incense and ebony wood from Sub-Saharan Africa were **traded,** to Egypt and civilizations throughout the Mediterranean; and for about 100 years **conquered** and ruled Egypt's 25th Dynasty. They knew they couldn't cover-up was deliberately bye-passed; by a racist historian's threat, to **Nubian American's** world history.

Now here's where the evil and **"racist hate"** comes in at. They've been **taught** as a child, to take a black man's **life** doesn't matter; especially a racist white-police, who gets away with it!!! They think we're "nothing," until they learn **kinky-hair Nubian Americans** are the same **pre-history** people whose ancestors had a civilization, whose rulers built temples; while white racist at the same time like any animal living in **caves,** had no intellect, a must be known to them. And claiming white supremacy, doesn't remove an **uncivilized cave-man savage** instinct. **"Racism,"** is destroying the world; ever since they created it some 600 years ago. However, when **Nubian American's Rise,** America will be **saved** to go to her **Black** Israel's **"chosen people"** prophesy...

Just like, the ancient over 2,000 years old **"Baghdad Dry Cell Batteries,"** a Euro-U.S. & Jew's unbelievable, in envy perhaps but "not **forgotten,**" by bigot sophisticated scholars of deceptions ready-made policy of a racist society. It didn't fit in with the mainstream established viewpoint, who hoped would go away like **mixing** Israel did. Electricity was made out a pottery jar, copper sheet, vinegar the likely acid, asphalt, and an iron electrode. And **Israel** is not white-Jews **home.**

Just like chiseled in **stone,** the temple of Seti I's hieroglyphs in **Abydos,** black **Kemet** (Egypt), **3,000 years old** ancient helicopter, submarine and airplanes depicting "modern-tech." or the monumental **Nubian "first"** world figures, carved out of mountainous stone (Mount Rushmore imitated), is **Abu Simbel,** "The Rock Temple in **Nubia** (Cush)," are about **pre-histories legacies of rulers.** Ancient **Nubian's** better way of life **lessons;** is *that old kind religion,* will heal & inspire   economics "growth & prosperity" for the *struggling* is the **Nubian American identity,** a today's **census registry.** A *Fortney Encyclical History Ed. Co.'s,* "Thank You."

"WE ARE PROVEN NUBIAN AMERICANS"

To begin with, at a news conference in December of 1988 at Chicago's Hyatt Regency O' Hare Hotel, it was said leaders of "75 black groups" met, and with Rev. Jessy Jackson, a new national black agenda of being called "African American," was accomplished.

The Rev. Jessy Jackson said, "To be called African-Americans has cultural integrity," "it puts us in our proper "historical context;" then most certainly, what more when historical context describe cultural heredity identity…" There's no limit with more that define as being **"Nubian Americans,"** and what it does to a certain **"tribal nation"** of people distinguished by their important trait of physicality; and that being **kinky wooly-hair** like **lamb's wool** and skin like **burnt bronze,** biblical description is today's **Nubian Americans** whites hate to give recognition.

If a national survey, the polls would likely show their great numbers with **dignity** and **pride,** what Black peoples want to be called is **Nubian Americans** is their **"heritage"** from the **African Continent.** This the new term to replace the African Americans term, with the preferred Nubian Americans acceptance; among doubters opinion makers there's Africa's Nubia **DNA, that will quite any objections,** a powerful imagery of a political exercise in naming, to the national press. We recalled the imposition of "Black" over "Negro," then became "African American," now a recall to become called, a Nubian American's **"proper world-wide known identity."**

We redefine ourselves, Nubian Americans to gain back our ancient **pre-history** ancestors just do respect and to educate the today's racist hate society, that destroys with evil and kills the unarmed innocent black-man. Has held us to be an inferior random and sub-human to their white supremacy agenda, it almost seems, allowing title-tags without specific identity to be the norm. Reconstruction era as humiliating and even vengeful imposing to them and not wanted.

Recently, hundreds of news organizations have changed back to a Black tag in reference to the old struggle and race of us kinky wooly-hair people who trace their ancestry to Africa; strikes deeper to Nubian Americans who were <u>stripped</u> of their "<u>bye-passed</u> identity" and <u>enslaved</u>. Denied of speaking their motherland tongue of Nubian, who were known worldwide in **"trading."** We now pay homage to a recall, a rightfully deserved that people **"gains,"** many Nubian Americans has shed their **blood** for.

This asks an important question, but what is white historians excuse for <u>bypassing</u>, <u>over</u>-<u>looking</u> and just plain **"<u>hiding</u>,"** knowledge from all American student's education, of Nubian history who once ruled in ancient Egypt? Would greatly lessen stupidity or help to eliminate his <u>racist's</u> doings. **Nubia,** is home to civilization's older than the dynastic Egyptians, evade the Nile River in what is today's northern **Sudan** and southern Egypt was purposely paid relatively little attention. However, Nubian history is often intertwined with Egypt's to the north.

Racism, and/is a rediscovery by Nubian Americans of Ancient Nubia even to the architect of the pyramid. Although different in statue and build and created earlier than the famed great Egyptian pyramids of Giza, Sudan has more pyramids than Egypt. There are around **2,000** Kushite (Cushite Nubian) pyramids in upper Sudan, compared with 200 Egyptian pyramids. Hence, Nubian history was <u>ignored</u> because it was not European white-man's history like <u>whitewashed</u> Egypt is.

Plus, due to the **fact,** that <u>racist</u> archaeologist and <u>bigoted</u> white historians actually <u>dismissed</u> the idea of black Africans were capable of creating anything artistic, of technology, or cities like those from Egypt, Greece or Rome. Nubia's **<u>Negroes</u>,** were a mere extension of

Egypt with a few paragraphs on black pharaohs at best, if that much. We will no longer tolerate, **wrong!**!!

Nubian study, a "magnificent historical significance," for **Nubian Americans** and all other students for *high learning* was rejected, for white supremacy control in power, with the fear of a black-people take over aggression. However, **Africa's** history emphatically says, **Ethiopia** is the *"Grandmother,"* **Nubia** the *"Mother"* and **Egypt** is the *"child."* This is the **"beginning"** of all of civilization's history, no matter how they the outsider try to distort, a beautiful honest *"Truth."*

Black, was the common understanding until Europeans painted Biblical characters **white;** to able him without hateful envy in spite to worship them, and not the **"spirit of God;"** having everyone glorify and praise the white man as if God, because he couldn't in "God's" true image. Ham had a son named **Cush,** which means **black** in **Hebrew.** Cush is the most common usage designating color, referring to people, persons or lands used in the Bible. It is used **"58 times"** in the King James Version. The Greek/Latin word is **Ethiopia.** In classical literature, **Greek** and **Roman** authors describe Ethiopians as "Black."

The Nubia DNA can be explained in Genesis 10:6-20 that describes the descendants of ham as being located in North, Central, South Africa and southern **Asia.** Psalm 105:23 mentions the "Land of Ham" in Egypt, and Psalm 78:51 connects the "tents of Ham" with Egypt. In Genesis 10, Nimrod, son of Cush, whose name means black, founded a civilization in **Mesopotamia.** The Egyptians (Ham), are **"genetically"** linked to **Sub-Saharan Nubians.** The **Romans** record that there were "Black People" in **Britain** (White Man's prehistory) and other parts of Europe, when they first encountered them.

"ANCIENT NUBIAN 6,000 YRS. OLD GOLD ECONOMICS STUDY"

Ancient 6,000 years old economics of the Nubian gold trade alone, should have promulgated, is a spearheaded histories top of the list need; for **K-12 Nubian History Schoolhouse Learning** in education that to the south of Egypt was "Rich and Powerful **Nubia;**" and not <u>excluded,</u> built on the **devil's** advocate of "**white supremacy's** <u>fraud</u> and <u>fear</u>." Not only is <u>racist</u> <u>hate attacks</u> <u>killing</u> innocent **"Nubian Americans,"** has killed by erasing Nubian history from our minds except relayed coming from "Kings and Queens." We will **"rise"** soon, what we attempt with the topic of Nubia's **ancient gold,** like Nubian Christ's eternal glorious **resurrection...**

Just as, now we learn, through the gold trade's **6,000 years,** that **Nubian** history is before the mistaken **Sumerians.** Our golden history, relates to the **Nile River** (the Gihon river as known in the Holy Bible), that goes through Uganda, the Sudan, and extends from northern Kenya to the Mediterranean Sea is a total of **3,485 miles.** The **longest** river, "in the world." Just as the so-called Middle-East (Asia Minor), is actually of the Nubian Continent's, **"Northeast Africa."**

A once one land mass, before the [so-called] disconnect digging of the Suez Canal in 1869. And the region of Mesopotamia, which included Assyria and **Babylonia** (Iraq is now located), were the original jet black **"Hamites and Shemites,"** also, Hebrew original **black Jews.** The name of Jesus in Hebrew is **Ye-shu-ah,** which means, "one who shall save by righteous teachings and example" (Matthew 3:15).

Ancient 6,000 years of gold mining in the Eastern Deserts of Egypt and Nubia/Sudan are located in the crystalline basement east of the Nile and primarily bound to quartz veins. Nubia, particularly rich in gold deposits, was an important envied conquest for the ancient Egyptians. **"Gold mines,"** which some of them were under Egyptian control can be proven in **Nubia**. Gold bearing quartz chunks due to erosion were collected by hundreds of workers, then processed in Wadis dry valleys of the mountains. They call it, "wadiworkings."

Ancient Nubia's location was so ideal for trade. The Nile River was the route to Egypt and rich port cities circumference of the Mediterranean Sea. Ancient Nubia had access in the east to the Red Sea, opening up trade to the Arabian Peninsula, the southern east coast of Africa and ports farther away. By the time of Egypt's First Dynasty, **international trade** was with regions of the Levant (Israel), Libya, and Nubia. Egypt had a trading colony in Canaan, a number of them in Syria, but even more in **Nubia**. The overland trade route was through the Wadi Hammamat from the Nile to the Red Sea, then goods traveled on the "backs of donkeys."

Many of these trade agreements were achieved through peaceful negotiation, and some were established by military campaigns on both sides. Nubia was rich in gold mines and gets its name in fact, from the Egyptian word for gold, **Nub.** There were many trade centers in Nubia however, one of the most important of them referred to in Egyptian text was **"Yam."** During the Old Kingdom of Nubia (2613-2118 BC), Yam was noted for its **ebony** hard wood (reddish brown and black), **ivory,** and **gold,** location of Yam precisely is unknown however, it is thought to have been somewhere in the **"Shendi Reach"** area of the Nile River in modern-day **Sudan.**

Cush's (Nubia) location and natural resources made it an important trading junction or a center. Ancient Nubia linked central and southern Africa to Egypt. Black Egyptian Pharaohs sent expeditions on ships south along the Nile River to buy, or sometimes a <u>raid</u> to <u>steal</u>, goods. But however the deal, Egyptians traded wheat grain and linen cloth for Nubian's precious gold, ivory, leather, and timber.

During Byzantine times, the **Bedouin tribes,** who dominated the entire Eastern Desert as tradition would have it, were not interested in mining (still are today), refused any kind of digging in the ground; even agriculture in watered, Wadi grounds. However in contrast, in Northeast Sudan away from areas close to the Nile River, many new sites were started in secondary gold deposits of Wadi working operations.

Of all the many known Pharaonic gold producing sites in Egypt and Northeast Sudan, the history surely about 6,000 years tradition in gold producing, however, less than the monthly output of gold was achieved of present day South Africa; which was still a lot of gold back then.

The total tonnage of all mined ancient trenches and underground operations was estimated to the order of 400,000 to 600,000 tons of quartz ore. Figuring a recovery of 10 grams/a ton, is about $2/3^{rd}$ the maximum concentration mined, a maximum of 6,000 kilograms of Au grade is yielded. One kg (kilogram) of gold ='s 1,000 9 (grams), and today's 1 kilo ='s 2.2 pounds or $59,372.8 x 6,000 kilos is $356,236 **million** dollars times 5 the value at least the ancient past; ='s 1 trillion, 881 billion, 180 million, 000, 000 dollars or $1,881,180,000,000 dollars **"6,000 years ago,** that lasted about, almost a **thousand** years.

As Egypt became bigger they desired much more **"luxury goods"** such as **gold, animal skins, gemstones** and **perfumes.** They established a trade relationship with ancient Nubia to obtain gold the Egyptians needed for more exotic wood and Nubians needed grain to survive, the Egyptians had. And besides other African Kingdoms and Arabia, Nubia also traded with distant **Rome,** of Italy, **India,** and even **China.** The largest, wealthy ancient Nubian city of **Meroe,** was the hub, a center metropolis of Cushite civilization and gold trade at its height, lasted just about a **1,000** years. Nubian shield hosted around **250 gold mine** production **sites.**

And so today, with this blatant "white-supremacy" lie, and replacement theory running ramped, in America, no wonder anyone can clearly see why monumental statues of beautiful **"Nubian Kings and Queens,"** (many with wide nose and thick lips chipped away), and the magnificently carved **"Rock Temple of Abu Simbel,"** was meant to be absent, by bigoted Euro-Americans who avoided **Nubian** history. And brazenly, falsely-depicted as Egyptian; posing as the architect creator of **Africa's** "Great Pyramids," in schoolhouse studies world-history.

"GOLD," the yellow metal that captures the heart and some men souls, who'll take another's life… It is said that **gold** (money), is the "root" of all **evil**. However, there's an evil root "worst" than gold. The worst root said to be, is the worst lie ever told was there's no such thing as the **DEVIL**. And only an evil **devil**, as Nubian wooly-hair **Christ** emphasized the proof is in John 8:44, "Ye are of *your* father the devil…a liar and the father of it." Would lie and make it appear the scriptures great Cush (Nubian nation), the **first man** on earth was of **black skin** and **wooly hair** made in **God's image,** was the ones who **created** and **wrote** the **Holy Bible;** that their superb history **never existed!** Nubian history is **left-out** of white man's world history.

Not in any racist sense, but we were God's "chosen people" who'll return to **Israel** and not a people who fake to be us Rev. 2:9, "…say they are Jews, and are not, but *are* the synagogue of Satan." This is astutely recognized, and pointed-out with no harm intended; in a provocative positive sense, only to inspire. **Nubian Africa's "black man's golden-history,"** wrote the **Bible** that European whites revised. They depict with racist overtones, all major original kinky wooly hair black characters in text book study and **Hollywood's** Jewish owned filming industry; they've whitewashed as all white, except always with us as demeaning servants or slaves are the **"black Africans** or **Nubian Americans."**

The grand historian author of the *Fortney Encyclical History Ed. Co.,* is bent on everyone having the correct knowledge with learning and an honest **understanding** and **"lessons of wisdom,"** from an array of our company books. The future is our precious children. We must teach & instruct all our children at an early age; by showing them a pattern to live by not acting the <u>fool</u>, but in the **right**-way for peace and harmony, for all races to live together and **co-exist.**

We together must take care of this **planet,** it's the only one we have to live on. Because it's a known fact of death that, no worldly goods and no amount of **gold** or money can you take with you, once leaving here forever. And so, having nowhere else to go we must all clean the earth, water, and air from pollutants, but most of all our **"minds"** from the pollutants of <u>hate</u> and <u>racism</u> toward a more **righteous thinking,** whatever your spiritual belief.

Nubia Region Today Map

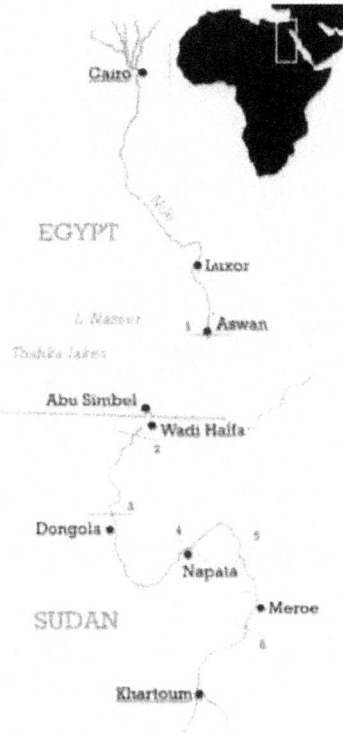

Nubia was also called - Upper & Lower Nubia, Kush, Land of Kush, Te-Nehesy, Nubadae, Napata, or the Kingdom of Meroe.

The region referred to as Lower Egypt is the northernmost portion. Upper Nubia extends south into Sudan and can be subdivided into several separate areas such as Batn El Hajar or "Belly of Rocks", the sands of the Abri-Delgo Reach, or the flat plains of the Dongola Reach. Nubia, the hottest and most arid region of the world, has caused many civilizations to be totally dependent on the Nile for existence.

Nubian Meroe Pyramids

Ramesses II Storming the Hittite Fortres of Dapur. Meroe people were Kushite, Nubia who rule 25th Dynasty Egypt

The Great Nubian is Before the Egyptians

**The Giza plateau 3 predominant Pyramids & Great Sphinx
Lower left, The Great Sphinx face east**

25th Nubian Dynasty/Kushite Tadja made of Ivory 760-656BC

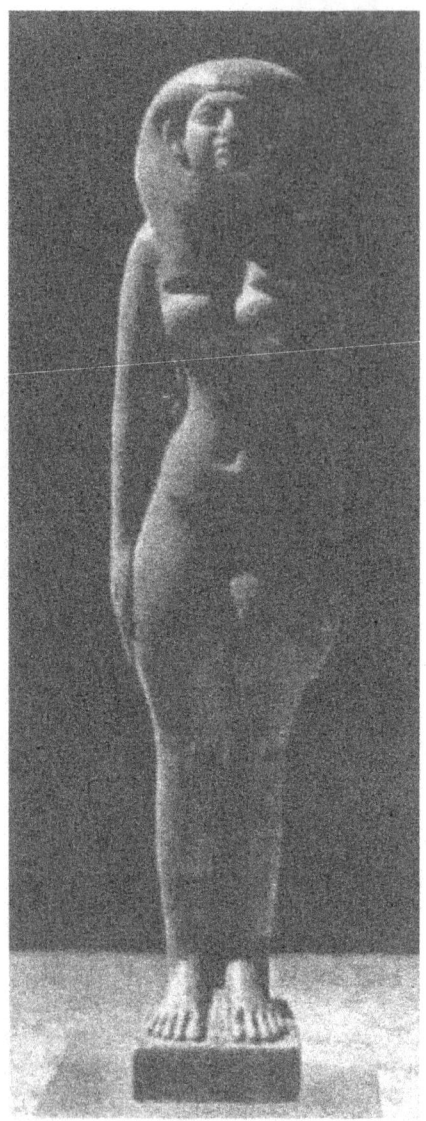

Nubian Winged Goddess 743-712BC Earthenware

"WOOLY-HAIR CHRIST WAS A BLACK NUBIAN"

Nubian American's great Africa's past, cannot be hidden or chipped away wide black nose and beautiful thick lips in white man's "envy explorations" to <u>steal</u> land, religion and history in the name of **"<u>evil</u>."** And with, <u>anti-black</u> <u>hate-groups</u> in fear of losing their **white**-**supremacy** <u>lie</u> along with their "<u>replacement</u> <u>theory</u>" excuse to *practice* **"<u>genocide</u>"** on others, brings to light the "motherland of humanity" is the sacred black color of **Africa,** and her Black form of **God** is only **natural;** welcomed **"rediscovery"** of our **Nubian American selves.** Because to "love a White version" of our Black God of Christ, is to *subconsciously* <u>despise</u> or <u>hate</u> your Black-self.

A shrine to the **Black Madonna** and the **Prince of peace,** is the word **Christ,** comes from Indian, Krishna or Chrishna, which means "the Black one." The Egyptian God Osiris, the Krishnas of India; the Buddhas of India, Japan and China; the Xaha of Japan; Laotsze of China; the Fuhi of China; the Sommonacom of Siam; the ancient Druid gods; and the gods of Greece were **Black.** Black Grecia gods included were Apollo, Baccus, Jupiter, Hercules, and Ammon; and the goddesses Isis, Venus Junno, Metis, Hecati, Cybele and Ceres were all worshipped in Rome of Italy. **<u>Original</u> <u>author</u> <u>of</u> <u>the</u> "<u>HOLY</u> <u>BIBLE</u>" <u>were</u> <u>kinky</u> <u>wool</u>-<u>hair</u> <u>African</u> <u>Nubians</u>.**

A white Christ encourages subservience of Black people to whites, who occupy most all Americans political seats of authority, and the Nubian American is our model only we can embody correctly, ours without fault of **identity.** Blackness is an **"*essence*"** structure of realities **"first."** Because, a Black people who allow white others to determine their image with a white God will allow and go for anything of others to "control" our women and children, goods, economic resources, and necessities of Black lives. **Images**

always go much deeper than words.

Do not fear Black Christ. Perhaps **Hollywood's** objective, with **dark** looking **devils** or **black monsters** looking human like in their movies; that sub-consciously *all children minds* will fear Black-people, are **"genocide hate set-ups,"** with **monster movies; Satan's** *reverse* tricknology; whites conveniently always looking right on screen. And sub-consciously, many black women may burn in hell; an abomination of longing to be in the arms of an evil deceptive, and made-up blond hair, blue eyes idol, with an "All American white Christ," was the **Slave-master's** *dream* of reasoning; with psycho-sexual analytic theories, for his experimenting **breeding farms.**

Just as or like, the **"Great Wall of China,"** was built in the 14th through the 17th centuries A.D. during the Ming Dynasty and when European 15th century **"racism was created."** However, if China told it like it is, was to keep the trouble-makers, the northern-white nomadic tribes out of China from **invasion.** Most-likely China through trading with Nubian/Egyptians, were warned by either or both to keep them out. Build a wall, like we didn't have the chance too, perhaps hinted to China who kept in mind and did. What remains was mostly built in the Ming Dynasty (1368-1644). The average height is 20 to 23 feet tall, and the tallest section of the wall was 46 feet. The length of the great wall is **13,170.70** miles long. America's coast to coast is 3,100 miles.

Then there's the notion, perhaps China contemplated and saw what happened to **Africa's** Black Israelite **Jews,** by Whites who **say they are Jews and are not.** Said, **"The liberator Christ."**

And so, whatever it was, China decided and built her great wall on speculation or without, ever done in history, to keep an enemy out of China. Their anticipation was certain, and built with spaced watch-towers on top the wall to communicate any approach of the menace they feared, known to have a troubling history. A renowned white man once said, "Strong fences makes for good neighbors." And so, **proud** "new neighbors" are always **Nubian Americans. Amen.**

The dictionary definition of African American is "an American of Africa and especially of Black African descent;" but no important word such as **Nubian,** much less Nubian American is in any dictionary print… Then next, there's the word **"Afro:"** a hairstyle of tight curls in a full evenly rounded shape. White man's dictionary skipped over *global nickname* **Nubian** to Afro!

However, there is a term that truly describes with all kinds of proof, (aside from school-book learning), a people who were taken from Africa and forced into slavery and that term is properly called identity; which describes the unique kinky wooly-hair black-skin of distinction is the **"Nubian American;"** is the correction and not the African American per-se (as such). The term **"Nubia"** means to the many *"world-wide"* and *"in America,"* **it has come to be virtually synonymous with** *"Blackness"* **and** *Africa."* **Cush** (Nubia) is mentioned **"58" times** in the Bible.

In conclusion, Isaiah 18:2, referred the **Cushites** (Nubians) as a people "feared near and far," and a "nation mighty and conquering." This was the ancient **Nubian** (Cushite) "military reputation," in ancient Egypt and the Near East for the most part. It is also important to note: **Cush** (Kush), **Ethiopic** Nubians, **Sudanic** Nubians and **Egyptic** Nubians are same *stock* **"Nubia people's"** DNA military might, but also a **"land of wealth"** known for its *"precious stones."* Job mentions the *topaz* of Cush as being very valuable (Job 28:19). **"Israelite people's identity"** was **defined** by its relationship to **Yahweh (Christ),** the **God of Israel.** But not in **history** books?

Cush will experience Yahweh's **judgment** (Amos 9:8). The Bible is clear that **Nubia** [Cush's descendants, the Nubian Americans], are like ancient **Israel** [today's Palestinians and Nubians] who also will experience Christ's **salvation** (Zephaniah 3:10) and (Psalms 68:31), that was prophesized. America's Statue of Liberty and its relationship **"warnings,"** of Babylon (Rev. 17:1 to 18). **"Repent" America, do your job and "Rise" together with God's Nubian Americans!**

Nubian American Means Black Creativity. *"The mark of distinction."* Let's get *smarter* about *us*.

We would like to congratulate your book **"The Fortney Encyclical Black History: The World's True Black History"** as it has been appraised. From traditional publishers, they have given a promising **8.2** out of **10**. Although there remark is slightly confidential, you may be pleased to know that this is what the reviewers have said, *"The author weaves words together like a fine thread formulating ideas, relating scenes or images together exceptionally. The voice is pronounced and consistent, which is vital in any celebrated literary piece. These are the qualities that set the author apart from all other writers."* I hope you realize that this is exceptional material. It has captivated literary agents and, surely its future readers. A Senior Book Agent & Brand Manager from Scriptor House.

A **"Racial Standard with Hair"** is that, there's an emphasis concerning hair and the races we just can't ignore in closing. We start with the **Asian** Continent of **India's** black-skin people having **"straight"** black hair. Then there's the **Spanish Latino** very light brown-skin people having **"straight"** black hair. Then there's the **Chinese Asian** [so-called by Euro-historians] yellow-skin people having **"straight"** black hair. However, then there's the **African** largest continent of black-skin people **Nubian African** and the **North Americas Nubian American "kinky wooly"** black-hair distinction; are the only people or anywhere else let it be known, even with skin as light or lighter than brown people's skin, are the "only ones" who can claim this unique type hair in the world. *The Planet is On Fire…Climate-Change at point of no return!*

White man scholars of history can't <u>imitate</u> to follow-up or resemble as a model with **kinky wooly hair** to <u>whitewash</u> <u>history</u>, even after <u>chipping-away</u> black's big lips and wide noses of Nubian/Egyptians ancient representing statues and monument. And so, he <u>completely</u> **omitted** Nubia/Cush from **<u>his false</u>** 'world history and dictionary's.' Please note there are some original Ethiopians next door neighbors to Nubia with genetically straight hair; believed in prehistory migrated and settled as India's Asian beginning. This makes **"Kinky Wooly Hair"** having the important and vital, racial standard with a **"Hair's Mark of Distinction"** of a people.

We all know, if not can feel or heard what the White man's standard is in America that once made fun of and not in good jest but a <u>mockery</u>, of a hero unaware to Black folk. However, we saying in defense against that <u>mockery</u> in disguise of an **"unknowing hero."** So before we leave you, the last vital **lesson** aside from DNA, all Black folks must know that no matter how light towards White your skin, if you got our "hero" of **kinky wooly-hair** on top of your head to chin distinctively like Black skin, you **"Nubian American Family"** my brother of greatness that's in God's image what gets you in… And God bless America against White or Black <u>Racism</u> period.

"And Last But Not Least, For the Record," America can't have her cake and eat it too; you can't mix the righteous good with the <u>evil</u> bad all together and call it one with under God, and declare a freedom for its rights. God objects to His, "Biblical Rule of Laws" not up-held; with warnings to living in peaceful co-existing is either this or that; one way or the other; with no straddling the fence that "man marry woman & woman marry man" is perhaps the whole issue.

Directly from our <u>misuse</u> and <u>abuse</u> of God's **"gift of sexuality,"** stems a large percent of the world's problems that could be greatly reduced like; STD's Aids, divorce, fatherless children, incest, sex trafficking, rape etc… If **"God's"** rule of laws were "upheld and obeyed," of His sexuality standards, disease would drop immensely world-wide, economy would rise and most all mental hospitals would have empty beds if we all sought to live within the healthy practice God instructed to do. Same sex marriage **denounce God** is an unthinkable **evil** act in His name?

Not only to **procreate,** but vitally important **ancestral traits,** are handed down through generations such as: intelligence, mannerism, physical structural appearance, and personality. God's pleasure is real, and man and woman in marriage of coming together as one is truly satisfying; Satan, and his devils counterfeit joys of folly, is empty and destructive with pleasure; because **chromosome genetic traits,** are transmitted through **"God's gift"** of **sexual pleasure in marriage** when "sperm meets egg as one." *Woman* is *part* of *man* making them *one* in *marriage*.

This is God's most outstanding rule of law in *"nature;"* protected with His stern penalties regardless; to those that anything other, support blasphemy liberty; an **atheistic** mockery idea to an ungodly freedom under democracy, period. Same sex marriage is **White man's** American creation. The last shall be first is the Nubian Americans in a turmoil wilderness America, whose ancestors created and practiced, a *"first democracy"* in **Northeast Africa's** *"Nubian Empires."*

"The Bible Speaks" – 1 Peter 4:11. **"America is Calling Evil…Good"** Isaiah 5:20 – Woe unto them that call evil good, and good evil; that put darkness for light, and lightness for darkness; that put bitter for sweet, and sweet for bitter. Hebrews 13:4 – Marriage *is* honorable in all, and the bed undefiled: but whoremongers and adulterers God will judge. And, Isaiah 5:24. God did not make homosexuals; it is **not** a DNA genetic trait, their actions are a result of their own lust and evil desires – James 1:13-14. Sometimes forced upon one (the hell of prison). **HELP THEM!**

Hebrew 13:3 – Remember them who are in prison, as though in prison with them, and them which suffer [hard times], since you also...**Same sex marriage goes against God's Black image!!**

If YOU are guilty of homosexuality and lesbianism, we urge you to be washed, be sanctified, and quit this sinful practice – Romans 1:16, Mark 16:16; Acts 2:38; 1 Corinthians 6:11. This isn't a **"religious hyperbole"** – extravagant exaggeration used as a figure of speech, just to influence; this is truth, honor, integrity, with liberty and salvation is **"Real LOVE to Live By with SOUL."**

America is somewhat like, biblical **Babylon.** The setting of the **Holy Bible** all took place in **Northeast Africa,** despite political constructs of so-called (originated in America) Middle East and western Asia. They don't want to credit Black-skinned people with *"intelligence,"* a racist agenda. And the Bible does not differentiate race; it only differentiates **nationalities** and **tribes. Acts 17: 26 And hath made of one blood all nations of men...** *Nubians are Gods chosen people.*

Today's **fascist** right wing conservative's ideology called "Trump Republicans," seem to have as nature's DNA characteristic, with a negative **evil** genetic trait. Racist White-Supremacist modern-day **Satan** was Hitler, now is protégé **Satan** Trump, to **anti-Christ** Putin then America's Republican Senate **coup** with a dangerous **demonic** ideology, won't change with bad laws that:

1. You want kids to have weapons of mass destruction, as a **demand** of your **oath** of office??
2. You **kicked** God out of our schools, now why you want kids **raped** to have the children??
3. You want climate change that's destroying the planet earth is a global **EMERGANCY.**
4. You want **"lies"** that can take the lives or kill black and brown to dominate the House & Senate with the courts that also threatens. With **unaccountable** racist white police

killings of blacks with nothing done but frivolous investigations lead to no prosecution, as justice.
5. You want laws to gerrymander the vote and ruin democracy, and control all evil sorts of **power.** You're America's creator of same sex marriage a *right* to an *evil oath,* under **God??**
6. You want your knee to continue strangling on the necks of the poor, pay high taxes while the wealthy corporations pay nothing expanding their gluttonous **'profit'** practices. Satan Semite with no empathy no mercy **beware** biting **you,** creating a **blackman** devil's **wrath.**
7. You reject law enforcement accountability to racist acts that kill black and brown people. With some **police** secretly acting out, within the benevolent association in **cowardice** to **murder,** and conspire in a secret unspoken oath, to pagan sacrilegious sacrificing of even children, much less black people is standard ritual for them and their **Satanic-cult/coup.**
8. You want Nubian Americans kept in a form of servitude without resource power.
9. You want the Black man's **Nubian** American's *"cultural and ancestral heritage history,"* taught in education continued being inexcusably denied is pure evil that may be criminal.

While Democracy advocates godly good DNA genetic characteristics that **must stop** the lies, destruction and death like todays **"Satan's Little Israel;"** in the **"Ancient Black man's Nubian Holy Land City of Jerusalem,"** with "Today's White man's blasphemy gay parades & civil-war massacres" to the likes of trying to make a "Big Israel America." As justice ignores our "jus tice" as was with a **patriate,** the **Nubian liberator** *Jesus,* who was crucified then and is now **"jes us."**

Truly our **'aim'** is telling about *"truth, trust* and *love,"* certainly a DNA's *identity* issue that's definitely not meant to harm, hurt nor debase; only relaying of **"God's"** absolute, *"messages and warnings,"* in the holy scriptures and out. Stay **mentally strong, alert** and hold-fast to the ethnic origin of the "Jews" lesson again, is **Hebrew Africa's** Black people. As the Bible indicates, it's in their Euro-Semite **nature.** It's in their DNA characteristic genetic trait as liars, to the death of others against all other **better** tribes and nations; explains why, "I know thy works... I *know* the blasphemy of them which say they are Jews, and are not, but *are* the synagogue of Satan.

    "It can't be emphasized enough, that the issues of human diversity "racial differences," is only "0.1 percent." Racial differences, didn't even exist prior to Caucasians using various color codes to create a societal hierarchy (persons arrange in a grade series), that was during "The Middle Ages" renaissance so-called artistic period (created the racist skin-color of differences) of the 15th century. Ancient Nubians nor Egyptians never referred to one another as "black," or "brown," or "white." People were just people and the color difference **"like from the gods,"** didn't matter. People were judged solely by the content of their character, deeds and **tribal** culture or **nationhood.** This means there was **No** race or color associated with people.

    But, by dividing people into various shades, Caucasian and Jews practice a "divide and rule" or **conquer** method. Just like with the new **"outer-space alien"** intervention into ancient history, use as a **method** to "undermine" hiding behind their created **"artistic license law,"** just because you can with **"Hollywood filming"** and at the head of the **"boards of education,"** won't rectify no restriction laws is just **wrong** and **"reveals"** *what* they truly are! To know who they are go to **John 8:44,** that speaks of his father the devil, the lusts he will do, he was a murderer, adode not in truth a liar and the father of it. However, *who* they truly are is in **Rev. 2:9,** all the best to you.

And so, this is their way to erase history that attacks and offend **Nubian American awareness,** divide with an undefined African American **title** (a rank, designation) is not **identity.** Just as **"Jew"** is their **"created title"** and not their true, original **identity** (the fact of being the same person or thing as claimed). By being **Euro**-Semite is proof enough of their Hebrew **fakery;** and not Biblical **Abraham's** Hebrew Nubian **stock** (Family, original), which is **"The Land of the Gods"** that even includes "Biblical Northeast Africa's **Israel,"** was once a part of the continent **Africa. "Reach-out, be kind and care more for each other."** You don't have to love but respecting each other's history is mandatory to co-exist! *"History gonna be made over."*

The majority of Black and most White folks, are **ignorant** to the **"facts"** and don't have any basic knowledge, don't know about the **NUBIAN AMERICAN** Black man or Black peoples true history; or essential things for both to get along is purposely kept from them knowing, *is Satan.* Racism along with the White Supremacy **hoax,** is a big-time money making indirect billionaires idea, scheme, 'method & sins' of an underhanded American industry. This vital book, *NUBIAN AMERICAN Identity Rise DNA PROOF,* is GOD'S **"wake-up call"** to America is **REPENT,** to the only healing remedy. Stay **mentally strong** no fade-outs or **die, confront** the issue to **heal** it!

In the beginning, there was only the mighty black man, and almighty God created [all] in Africa, and much time went by before the white man was created but not in Africa. **Nubia** in Africa had the **Hebrew Bible,** while uncivilized and living in caves, called a **"cave man"** white **Europeans** were pagan heathens called **gentiles.** Black and White K-12 students must be taught the *same* in school that starts with **Ethiopia...** *"In the beginning,"* then **Nubia,** and *last* ancient **Egypt.** In this chronological order of **culture,** the way it actually was in history and not starting with Egypt, enabling to deceive as the white man's civilization. This is our last chance from evil hate, an EMERGANCY for **TRUTH** to **"SAVE OUR CHILDREN"** that will give the best **insight** removing "bigoted problems and obstacles" that obstruct the black students **"best interest"** to learn of **their** heritage, and not European **misgivings**. Teach ALL our precious children is first a history of *high-tech* **sciences** like a, **"Nubian Wakanda"** of **"The DNA Great Gods of Africa."**

"Nubian Americans" – Fortney Encyclical History Ed. Co.'s Grand historian author **Albert Fortney Jr.** – Sole proprietor Exec.,

Ms. Cynthia Byrd – Lovely Chief Executive Officer (C.E.O.).

The **history company** became a Fortney Encyclical History Ed. Co. in 8/01/2017; when the book, *"A Child's Short History Book – Black History Month African Study (In cartoon animal characters)"* by Albert Fortney Jr., became an international enterprise; as/for an educational [non-profit] company, when copies were sent in 12/09/2014 to **Africa's** Oprah Winfrey Academy for girls. The book is also known, sent to the state of New Jersey's Senator Honorable Mr. Cory Booker and interstate sent to Mr. Kanye West, a recognized African American entertainer.

P.S. (Postscript), Democrat's DNA traits must fix the Supreme Court's Republican coup 6 to 3 justices advantage by expanding the court to 13, will protect the constitution in policy-making-decisions; then, the **electoral college** and the **filibuster,** both must be eliminated to protect democracy period! In order to pass a bill in the Senate, you must end the debate on it. Objecting to end the debate is called a filibuster. And 60 senators must vote to end debate, for the bill to proceed. DNA **Big Lie** is Satan father of lies Ashkenazi Jew Trump seen insurrection.

Filibuster **reform** would make it possible to pass legislation with less than 60 votes. We Nubian Americans **oppose** "filibuster reform" because it would severely backfire conveniently for "Black and Brown Progressivism," just as it already has with the 3 newly elected Supreme Court Justices Roe decision. President Mr. Biden has said he is "not a fan" of packing the court. Don't be a fan be a president and stop stalling to right the court along with House speaker Nancy Pelosi, D-Calif., told reporters that she has "no plans to bring it to the floor, " "I don't know that's a good idea..." but it's a <u>bad</u> and a <u>wrong idea</u> to just <u>foot</u>-<u>dragging</u> and loose!

    We must make sure our DNA of democracy doesn't ever again elect a candidate who loses the popular vote. The constitution assigns each state a number of *electors* based on the **"state's population."** The total number of electors is **538,** so anyone getting **"270"** of those *Electoral College votes* become *"president"* **regardless** of the popular vote.

    "Amending the constitution," requires a two-thirds vote by the House and the Senate plus approval by three-fourths of state legislatures would be too hard to get however, the *Electoral College* can become *irrelevant* **without** a constitutional amendment. Here's how: **Article 2** of the Constitution says states with a total of no less than 270 electors can agree to **"award"** all their electoral votes go to the presidential candidate who wins the **"popular vote."** And with this **automatically,** the winner of the popular vote gets the Electoral College votes to be **president**!!! Already 10 states and the District of Columbia have passed laws awarding all their electoral votes to the candidate who wins the popular vote when the 270 electoral is met.

    All together these states at present total 165 electoral say no votes. We now need additional states with 105 electoral votes agreeing to reward electoral votes to the popular vote and when that's done, never again will anyone become president who loses the popular vote. This endeavor is known as the "National Popular Vote Interstate Compact," and check to make sure your state has joined if it hasn't as yet please make sure it does! Nubian American DNA must get involved and employed in politics locally, county, state, and federal government **correct DNA education** in legislation for student's social studies history learning, with "Africa Curriculum Studies" **"colored-in with Black people's pictured history,"** and not Whites!

The New Yorker

A Critic at Large   July 20, 2020 Issue

The Invention of the Police

Why did American policing get so big, so fast? The answer, mainly, is slavery.

By Jill Lepore
July 13, 2020

To police is to maintain law and order, but the word derives from *polis*—the Greek for "city," or "polity"—by way of *politia*, the Latin for "citizenship," and it entered English from the Middle French *police*, which meant not constables but government. "The police," as a civil force charged with deterring crime, came to the United States from England and is generally associated with monarchy—"keeping the king's peace"—which makes it surprising that, in the antimonarchical United States, it got so big, so fast. The reason is, mainly, slavery.

"Abolish the police," as a rallying cry, dates to 1988 (the year that N.W.A. recorded "Fuck tha Police"), but, long before anyone called for its abolition, someone had to invent the police: the ancient Greek polis had to become the modern police. "To be political, to live in a *polis*, meant that everything was decided through words and persuasion and not through force and violence," Hannah Arendt wrote in "The Human Condition." In the polis, men argued and debated, as equals, under a rule of law. Outside the polis, in households, men dominated women, children, servants, and slaves, under a rule of force. This division of government sailed down the river of time like a raft, getting battered, but also bigger, collecting sticks and mud. Kings asserted a rule of force over their subjects on the idea that their kingdom was their household. In 1769, William Blackstone, in his "Commentaries on the Laws of England," argued that the king, as "pater-familias of the nation," directs "the public police," exercising the means by which "the individuals of the state, like members of a well-governed family, are bound to conform their general behavior to the rules of propriety, good neighbourhood, and good manners; and to be decent, industrious, and inoffensive in their respective stations." The police are the king's men.

History begins with etymology, but it doesn't end there. The polis is not the police. The American Revolution toppled the power of the king over his people—in America, "the law is king," Thomas Paine wrote—but not the power of a man over his family. The power of the police has its origins in that kind of power. Under the rule of law, people are equals; under the rule of police, as the legal theorist Markus Dubber has written, we are not. We are more like the women, children, servants, and slaves in a household in ancient Greece, the people who were not allowed to be a part of the polis. But for centuries, through struggles for independence, emancipation, enfranchisement, and equal rights, we've been fighting to enter the polis. One way to think about "Abolish the police," then, is as an argument that, now that all of us have finally clawed our way into the polis, the police are obsolete.

But are they? The crisis in policing is the culmination of a thousand other failures—failures of education, social services, public health, gun regulation, criminal justice, and economic development. Police have a lot in common with firefighters, E.M.T.s, and paramedics: they're there to help, often at great sacrifice, and by placing themselves in harm's way. To say that this doesn't always work out, however, does not begin to cover the size of the problem. The killing of George Floyd, in Minneapolis, cannot be wished away as an outlier. In each of the past five years, police in the United States have killed roughly a thousand people. (During each of those same years, about a hundred police officers were killed in the line of duty.) One study suggests that, among American men between the ages of fifteen and thirty-four, the number who were treated in emergency rooms as a result of injuries inflicted by police and security guards was almost as great as the number who, as pedestrians, were injured by motor vehicles. Urban police forces are nearly always whiter than the communities they patrol. The victims of police brutality are disproportionately Black teen-age boys: children. To say that many good and admirable people are police officers, dedicated and brave public servants, which is, of course, true, is to fail to address both the nature and the scale of the crisis and the legacy of centuries of racial injustice. The best people, with the best of intentions, doing their utmost, cannot fix this system from within.

There are nearly seven hundred thousand police officers in the United States, about two for every thousand people, a rate that is lower than the European average. The difference is guns. Police in Finland fired six bullets in all of 2013; in an encounter on a single day in the year 2015, in Pasco, Washington, three policemen fired seventeen bullets when they shot and killed an unarmed thirty-five-year-old orchard worker from Mexico. Five years ago, when the *Guardian* counted police killings, it reported that, "in the first 24 days of 2015, police in the US fatally shot more people than police did in England and Wales, combined, over the past 24 years." American police are armed to the teeth, with more than seven billion dollars' worth of surplus military equipment off-loaded by the Pentagon to eight thousand law-enforcement agencies since 1997. At the same time, they face the most heavily armed civilian population in the world: one in three Americans owns a gun, typically more than one. Gun violence undermines civilian life and debases everyone. A study found that, given the ravages of stress, white male police officers in Buffalo have a life expectancy twenty-two years shorter than that of the average American male. The debate about policing also has to do with all the money that's spent paying heavily armed agents of the state to do things that they aren't trained to do and that other institutions would do better. History haunts this debate like a bullet-riddled ghost.

That history begins in England, in the thirteenth century, when maintaining king's peace became the duty of an officer of the court called a constable, aided by his watchmen: every male adult could be called on to take a turn walking a ward at night and, if trouble came, to raise a hue and cry. This practice lasted for centuries. (A version endures: George Zimmerman, when he shot and killed Trayvon Martin, in 2012, was serving on his neighborhood watch.) The watch didn't work especially well in England—"The average constable is an ignoramus who knows little or nothing of the law," Blackstone wrote—and it didn't work especially well in England's colonies. Rich men paid poor men to take their turns on the watch, which meant that most watchmen were either very elderly or very poor, and very exhausted from working all day. Boston established a watch in 1631. New York tried paying watchmen in 1658. In Philadelphia, in 1705, the governor expressed the view that the militia could make the city safer than the watch, but militias weren't supposed to police the king's subjects; they were supposed to serve the common defense—waging wars against the French, fighting Native peoples who were trying to hold on to their lands, or suppressing slave rebellions.

The government of slavery was not a rule of law. It was a rule of police. In 1661, the English colony of Barbados passed its first slave law; revised in 1688, it decreed that "Negroes and other Slaves" were "wholly unqualified to be governed by the Laws . . . of our Nations," and devised, instead, a special set of rules "for the good Regulating and Ordering of them." Virginia adopted similar measures, known as slave codes, in 1680:

> It shall not be lawfull for any negroe or other slave to carry or arme himselfe with any club, staffe, gunn, sword or any other weapon of defence or offence, nor to goe or depart from of his masters ground without a certificate from his master, mistris or overseer, and such permission not to be granted but upon perticuler and necessary occasions; and every negroe or slave soe offending not haveing a certificate as aforesaid shalbe sent to the next constable, who is hereby enjoyned and required to give the said negroe twenty lashes on his bare back well layd on, and soe sent home to his said master, mistris or overseer . . . that if any negroe or other slave shall absent himself from his masters service and lye hid and lurking in obscure places, comitting injuries to the inhabitants, and shall resist any person or persons that shalby any lawfull

authority be imployed to apprehend and take the said negroe, that then in case of such resistance, it shalbe lawfull for such person or persons to kill the said negroe or slave soe lying out and resisting.

In eighteenth-century New York, a person held as a slave could not gather in a group of more than three; could not ride a horse; could not hold a funeral at night; could not be out an hour after sunset without a lantern; and could not sell "Indian corn, peaches, or any other fruit" in any street or market in the city. Stop and frisk, stop and whip, shoot to kill.

Then there were the slave patrols. Armed Spanish bands called *hermandades* had hunted runaways in Cuba beginning in the fifteen-thirties, a practice that was adopted by the English in Barbados a century later. It had a lot in common with England's posse comitatus, a band of stout men that a county sheriff could summon to chase down an escaped criminal. South Carolina, founded by slaveowners from Barbados, authorized its first slave patrol in 1702; Virginia followed in 1726, North Carolina in 1753. Slave patrols married the watch to the militia: serving on patrol was required of all able-bodied men (often, the patrol was mustered from the militia), and patrollers used the hue and cry to call for anyone within hearing distance to join the chase. Neither the watch nor the militia nor the patrols were "police," who were French, and considered despotic. In North America, the French city of New Orleans was distinctive in having *la police:* armed City Guards, who wore military-style uniforms and received wages, an urban slave patrol.

In 1779, Thomas Jefferson created a chair in "law and police" at the College of William & Mary. The meaning of the word began to change. In 1789, Jeremy Bentham, noting that "police" had recently entered the English language, in something like its modern sense, made this distinction: police keep the peace; justice punishes disorder. ("No justice, no peace!" Black Lives Matter protesters cry in the streets.) Then, in 1797, a London magistrate named Patrick Colquhoun published "A Treatise on the Police of the Metropolis." He, too, distinguished peace kept in the streets from justice administered by the courts: police were responsible for the regulation and correction of behavior and "the PREVENTION and DETECTION OF CRIMES."

It is often said that Britain created the police, and the United States copied it. One could argue that the reverse is true. Colquhoun spent his teens and early twenties in Colonial Virginia, had served as an agent for British cotton manufacturers, and owned shares in sugar plantations in Jamaica. He knew all about slave codes and slave patrols. But nothing came of Colquhoun's ideas about policing until 1829, when Home Secretary Robert Peel—in the wake of a great deal of labor unrest, and after years of suppressing Catholic rebellions in Ireland, in his capacity as Irish Secretary—persuaded Parliament to establish the Metropolitan Police, a force of some three thousand men, headed by two civilian justices (later called "commissioners"), and organized like an army, with each superintendent overseeing four inspectors, sixteen sergeants, and a hundred and sixty-five constables, who wore coats and pants of blue with black top hats, each assigned a numbered badge and a baton. Londoners came to call these men "bobbies," for Bobby Peel.

It is also often said that modern American urban policing began in 1838, when the Massachusetts legislature authorized the hiring of police officers in Boston. This, too, ignores the role of slavery in the history of the police. In 1829, a Black abolitionist in Boston named David Walker published "An Appeal to the Coloured Citizens of the World," calling for violent rebellion: "One good black man can put to death six white men." Walker was found dead within the year, and Boston thereafter had a series of mob attacks against abolitionists, including an attempt to lynch William Lloyd Garrison, the publisher of *The Liberator*, in 1835. Walker's words terrified Southern slaveowners. The governor of North Carolina wrote to his state's senators, "I beg you will lay this matter before the police of your town and invite their prompt attention to the necessity of arresting the circulation of the book." By "police," he meant slave patrols: in response to Walker's "Appeal," North Carolina formed a statewide "patrol committee."

New York established a police department in 1844; New Orleans and Cincinnati followed in 1852, then, later in the eighteen-fifties, Philadelphia, Chicago, and Baltimore. Population growth, the widening inequality brought about by the Industrial Revolution, and the rise in such crimes as prostitution and burglary all contributed to the emergence of urban policing. So did immigration, especially from Ireland and Germany, and the hostility to immigration: a new party, the Know-Nothings, sought to prevent immigrants from voting, holding office, and becoming citizens. In 1854, Boston disbanded its ancient watch and formally established a police department; that year, Know-Nothings swept the city's elections.

American police differed from their English counterparts: in the U.S., police commissioners, as political appointees, fell under local control, with limited supervision; and law enforcement was decentralized, resulting in a jurisdictional thicket. In 1857, in the Great Police Riot, the New York Municipal Police, run by the mayor's office, fought on the steps of city hall with the New York Metropolitan Police, run by the state. The Metropolitans were known as the New York Mets. That year, an amateur baseball team of the same name was founded.

Also, unlike their British counterparts, American police carried guns, initially their own. In the eighteen-sixties, the Colt Firearms Company began manufacturing a compact revolver called a Pocket Police Model, long before the New York Metropolitan Police began issuing service weapons. American police carried guns because Americans carried guns, including Americans who lived in parts of the country where they hunted for food and defended their livestock from wild animals, Americans who lived in parts of the country that had no police, and Americans who lived in parts of North America that were not in the United States. Outside big cities, law-enforcement officers were scarce. In territories that weren't yet states, there were U.S. marshals and their deputies, officers of the federal courts who could act as de-facto police, but only to enforce federal laws. If a territory became a state, its counties would elect sheriffs. Meanwhile, Americans became vigilantes, especially likely to kill indigenous peoples, and to lynch people of color. Between 1840 and the nineteen-twenties, mobs, vigilantes, and law officers, including the Texas Rangers, lynched some five hundred Mexicans and Mexican-Americans and killed thousands more, not only in Texas but also in territories that became the states of California, Arizona, Nevada, Utah, Colorado, and New Mexico. A San Francisco vigilance committee established in 1851 arrested, tried, and hanged people; it boasted a membership in the thousands. An L.A. vigilance committee targeted and lynched Chinese immigrants.

The U.S. Army operated as a police force, too. After the Civil War, the militia was organized into seven new departments of permanent standing armies: the Department of Dakota, the Department of the Platte, the Department of the Missouri, the Department of Texas, the Department of Arizona, the Department of California, and the Department of the Columbian. In the eighteen-seventies and eighties, the U.S. Army engaged in more than a thousand combat operations against Native peoples. In 1890, at Wounded Knee, South Dakota, following an attempt to disarm a Lakota settlement, a regiment of cavalrymen massacred hundreds of Lakota men, women, and children. Nearly a century later, in 1973, F.B.I. agents, SWAT teams, and federal troops and state marshals laid siege to Wounded Knee during a protest over police brutality and the failure to properly punish the torture and murder of an Oglala Sioux man named Raymond Yellow Thunder. They fired more than half a million rounds of ammunition and arrested more than a thousand people. Today, according to the C.D.C., Native Americans are more likely to be killed by the police than any other racial or ethnic group.

Modern American policing began in 1909, when August Vollmer became the chief of the police department in Berkeley, California. Vollmer refashioned American police into an American military. He'd served with the Eighth Army Corps in the Philippines in 1898. "For years, ever since Spanish-American War days, I've studied military tactics and used them to good effect in rounding up crooks," he later explained. "After all we're conducting a war, a war against the enemies of society." Who were those enemies? Mobsters, bootleggers, socialist agitators, strikers, union organizers, immigrants, and Black people.

To domestic policing, Vollmer and his peers adapted the kinds of tactics and weapons that had been deployed against Native Americans in the West and against colonized peoples in other parts of the world, including Cuba, Puerto Rico, and the Philippines, as the sociologist Julian Go has demonstrated. Vollmer instituted a training model imitated all over the country, by police departments that were often led and staffed by other veterans of the United States wars of conquest and occupation. A "police captain or lieutenant should occupy exactly the same position in the public mind as that of a captain or lieutenant in the United States army," Detroit's commissioner of police said. (Today's police officers are disproportionately veterans of U.S. wars in Iraq and Afghanistan, many suffering from post-traumatic stress. The Marshall Project, analyzing data from the Albuquerque police, found that officers who are veterans are more likely than their non-veteran counterparts to be involved in fatal shootings. In general, they are more likely to use force, and more likely to fire their guns.)

Vollmer-era police enforced a new kind of slave code: Jim Crow laws, which had been passed in the South beginning in the late eighteen-seventies and upheld by the Supreme Court in 1896. William G. Austin became Savannah's chief of police in 1907. Earlier, he had earned a Medal of Honor for his service in the U.S. Cavalry at Wounded Knee; he had also fought in the Spanish-American War. By 1916, African-American churches in the city were complaining to Savannah newspapers about the "whole scale arrests of negroes because they are negroes—arrests that would not be made if they were white under similar circumstances." African-Americans also confronted Jim Crow policing in the Northern cities to which they increasingly fled. James Robinson, Philadelphia's chief of police beginning in 1912, had served in the Infantry during the Spanish-American War and the Philippine-American War. He based his force's training on manuals used by the U.S. Army at Leavenworth. Go reports that, in 1911, about eleven per cent of people arrested were African-American; under Robinson, that number rose to 14.6 per cent in 1917. By the nineteen-twenties, a quarter of those arrested were African-Americans, who, at the time, represented just 7.4 per cent of the population.

Progressive Era, Vollmer-style policing criminalized Blackness, as the historian Khalil Gibran Muhammad argued in his 2010 book, "The Condemnation of Blackness: Race, Crime, and the Making of Modern Urban America." Police patrolled Black neighborhoods and arrested Black people disproportionately; prosecutors indicted Black people disproportionately; juries found Black people guilty disproportionately; judges gave Black people disproportionately long sentences; and, then, after all this, social scientists, observing the number of Black people in jail, decided that, as a matter of biology, Black people were disproportionately inclined to criminality.

More recently, between the New Jim Crow and the criminalization of immigration and the imprisonment of immigrants in detention centers, this reality has only grown worse. "By population, by per capita incarceration rates, and by expenditures, the United States exceeds all other nations in how many of its citizens, asylum seekers, and undocumented immigrants are under some form of criminal justice supervision," Muhammad writes in a new preface to his book. "The number of African American and Latinx people in American jails and prisons today exceeds the entire populations of some African, Eastern European, and Caribbean countries."

Policing grew harsher in the Progressive Era, and, with the emergence of state-police forces, the number of police grew, too. With the rise of the automobile, some, like California's, began as "highway patrols." Others, including the state police in Nevada, Colorado, and Oregon, began as the private paramilitaries of industrialists which employed the newest American immigrants: Hungarians, Italians, and Jews. Industrialists in Pennsylvania established the Iron and Coal Police to end strikes and bust unions, including the United Mine Workers; in 1905, three years after an anthracite-coal strike, the Pennsylvania State Police started operations. "One State Policeman should be able to handle one hundred foreigners," its new chief said.

The U.S. Border Patrol began in 1924, the year that Congress restricted immigration from southern Europe. At the insistence of Southern and Western agriculturalists, Congress exempted Mexicans from its new immigration quotas in order to allow migrant workers to enter the United States. The Border Patrol began as a relatively small outfit responsible for enforcing federal immigration law, and stopping smugglers, at all of the nation's borders. In the middle decades of the twentieth century, it grew to a national quasi-military focussed on policing the southern border in campaigns of mass arrest and forced deportation of Mexican immigrants, aided by local police like the notoriously brutal L.A.P.D., as the historian Kelly Lytle Hernández has chronicled. What became the Chicano movement began in Southern California, with Mexican immigrants' protests of the L.A.P.D. during the first half of the twentieth century, even as a growing film industry cranked out features about Klansmen hunting Black people, cowboys killing Indians, and police chasing Mexicans. More recently, you can find an updated version of this story in L.A. Noire, a video game set in 1947 and played from the perspective of a well-armed L.A.P.D. officer, who, driving along Sunset Boulevard, passes the crumbling, abandoned sets from D. W. Griffith's 1916 film "Intolerance," imagined relics of an unforgiving age.

Two kinds of police appeared on mid-century American television. The good guys solved crime on prime-time police procedurals like "Dragnet," starting in 1951, and "Adam-12," beginning in 1968 (both featured the L.A.P.D.). The bad guys shocked America's conscience on the nightly news: Arkansas state troopers barring Black students from entering Little Rock Central High School, in 1957; Birmingham police clubbing and arresting some seven hundred Black children protesting segregation, in 1963; and Alabama state troopers beating voting-rights marchers at Selma, in 1965. These two faces of policing help explain how, in the nineteen-sixties, the more people protested police brutality, the more money governments gave to police departments.

In 1965, President Lyndon Johnson declared a "war on crime," and asked Congress to pass the Law Enforcement Assistance Act, under which the federal government would supply local police with military-grade weapons, weapons that were being used in the war in Vietnam. During riots in Watts that summer, law enforcement killed thirty-one people and arrested more than four thousand; fighting the protesters, the head of the L.A.P.D. said, was "very much like fighting the Viet Cong." Preparing for a Senate vote just days after the uprising ended, the chair of the Senate Judiciary Committee said, "For some time, it has been my feeling that the task of law enforcement agencies is really not much different from military forces; namely, to deter crime before it occurs, just as our military objective is deterrence of aggression."

As Elizabeth Hinton reported in "From the War on Poverty to the War on Crime: The Making of Mass Incarceration in America," the "frontline soldiers" in Johnson's war on crime—Vollmer-era policing all over again—spent a disproportionate amount of time patrolling Black neighborhoods and arresting Black people. Policymakers concluded from those differential arrest rates that Black people were prone to criminality, with the result that police spent even more of their time patrolling Black neighborhoods, which led to a still higher arrest rate. "If we wish to rid this country of crime, if we wish to stop hacking at its branches only, we must cut its roots and drain its swampy breeding ground, the slum," Johnson told an audience of police policymakers in 1966. The next year, riots broke out in Newark and Detroit. "We ain't rioting agains' all you whites," one Newark man told a reporter not long before being shot dead by police. "We're riotin' agains' police brutality." In Detroit, police arrested more than seven thousand people.

Johnson's Great Society essentially ended when he asked Congress to pass the Omnibus Crime Control and Safe Streets Act, which had the effect of diverting money from social programs to policing. This magazine called it "a piece of demagoguery devised out of malevolence and enacted in hysteria." James Baldwin attributed its "irresponsible ferocity" to "some pale, compelling nightmare—an overwhelming collection of private nightmares." The truth was darker, as the sociologist Stuart Schrader chronicled in his 2019 book, "Badges Without Borders: How Global Counterinsurgency Transformed American Policing." During the Cold War, the Office of Public Safety at the U.S.A.I.D. provided assistance to the police in at least fifty-two countries, and training to officers from nearly eighty, for the purpose of counter-insurgency—the suppression of an anticipated revolution, that collection of private nightmares; as the O.P.S. reported, it contributed "the international dimension to the Administration's War on Crime." Counter-insurgency boomeranged, and came back to the United States, as policing.

In 1968, Johnson's new crime bill established the Law Enforcement Assistance Administration, within the Department of Justice, which, in the next decade and a half, disbursed federal funds to more than eighty thousand crime-control projects. Even funds intended for social projects—youth employment, for instance, along with other health, education, housing, and welfare programs—were distributed to police operations. With Richard Nixon, any elements of the Great Society that had survived the disastrous end of Johnson's Presidency were drastically cut, with an increased emphasis on policing, and prison-building. More Americans went to prison between 1965 and 1982 than between 1865 and 1964, Hinton reports. Under Ronald Reagan, still more social services were closed, or starved of funding until they died: mental hospitals, health centers, jobs programs, early-childhood education. By 2016, eighteen states were spending more on prisons than on colleges and universities. Activists who today call for defunding the police argue that, for decades, Americans have been defunding not only social services but, in many states, public education itself. The more frayed the social fabric, the more police have been deployed to trim the dangling threads.

The blueprint for law enforcement from Nixon to Reagan came from the Harvard political scientist James Q. Wilson between 1968, in his book "Varieties of Police Behavior," and 1982, in an essay in *The Atlantic* titled "Broken Windows." On the one hand, Wilson believed that the police should shift from enforcing the law to maintaining order, by patrolling on foot, and doing what came to be called "community policing." (Some of his recommendations were ignored: Wilson called for other professionals to handle what he termed the "service functions" of the police—"first aid, rescuing cats, helping ladies, and the like"—which is a reform people are asking for today.) On the other hand, Wilson called for police to arrest people for petty crimes, on the theory that they contributed to more serious crimes. Wilson's work informed programs like Detroit's STRESS (Stop the Robberies, Enjoy Safe Streets), begun in 1971, in which Detroit police patrolled the city undercover, in disguises that included everything from a taxi-driver to a "radical college professor," and killed so many young Black men that an organization of Black police officers demanded that the unit be disbanded. The campaign to end STRESS arguably marked the very beginnings of police abolitionism. STRESS defended its methods. "We just don't walk up and shoot somebody," one commander said. "We ask him to stop. If he doesn't, we shoot."

For decades, the war on crime was bipartisan, and had substantial support from the Congressional Black Caucus. "Crime is a national-defense problem," Joe Biden said in the Senate, in 1982. "You're in as much jeopardy in the streets as you are from a Soviet missile." Biden and other Democrats in the Senate introduced legislation that resulted in the Comprehensive Crime Control Act of 1984. A decade later, as chairman of the Senate Judiciary Committee, Biden helped draft the Violent Crime Control and Law Enforcement Act, whose provisions included mandatory sentencing. In May, 1991, two months after the Rodney King beating, Biden introduced the Police Officers' Bill of Rights, which provided protections for police under investigation. The N.R.A. first endorsed a Presidential candidate, Reagan, in 1980; the Fraternal Order of Police, the nation's largest police union, first endorsed a Presidential candidate, George H. W. Bush, in 1988. In 1996, it endorsed Bill Clinton.

Partly because of Biden's record of championing law enforcement, the National Association of Police Organizations endorsed the Obama-Biden ticket in 2008 and 2012. In 2014, after police in Ferguson, Missouri, shot Michael Brown, the Obama Administration established a task force on policing in the twenty-first century. Its report argued that police had become warriors when what they really should be is guardians. Most of its recommendations were never implemented.

In 2016, the Fraternal Order of Police endorsed Donald Trump, saying that "our members believe he will make America safe again." Police unions are lining up behind Trump again this year. "We will never abolish our police or our great Second Amendment," Trump said at Mt. Rushmore, on the occasion of the Fourth of July. "We will not be intimidated by bad, evil people."

Trump is not the king; the law is king. The police are not the king's men; they are public servants. And, no matter how desperately Trump would like to make it so, policing really isn't a partisan issue. Out of the stillness of the shutdown, the voices of protest have roared like summer thunder. An overwhelming majority of Americans, of both parties, support major reforms in American policing. And a whole lot of police, defying their unions, also support those reforms.

Those changes won't address plenty of bigger crises, not least because the problem of policing can't be solved without addressing the problem of guns. But this much is clear: the polis has changed, and the police will have to change, too. ♦

An earlier version of this piece misrepresented the number of Americans between the ages of fifteen and thirty-four who were treated as a result of police-inflicted injuries in emergency rooms.

Race, Policing, and Black Lives Matter Protests
- The death of George Floyd, in context.
- The civil-rights lawyer Bryan Stevenson examines the frustration and despair behind the protests.
- Who, David Remnick asks, is the true agitator behind the racial unrest?

- A sociologist examines the so-called pillars of whiteness that prevent white Americans from confronting racism.
- The Black Lives Matter co-founder Opal Tometi on what it would mean to defund police departments, and what comes next.
- The quest to transform the United States cannot be limited to challenging its brutal police.

Published in the print edition of the July 20, 2020, issue, with the headline "The Long Blue Line."

Jill Lepore, a staff writer at The New Yorker, is a professor of history at Harvard. Her books include "These Truths: A History of the United States" and "If Then: How the Simulmatics Corporation Invented the Future."

P.S. In Conclusion. "TRUMPISM Republicans," are boldly advocating and so blatantly arrogant that since Black man <u>slavery</u>, they now want to **<u>erase</u>** us Nubian and Brown peoples from the America Nubians built, it seems by any means necessary. Almost like Putin's Russia is trying to **<u>erase</u>** Ukrainians off the world's map! Is a fact, and an example is their new "<u>Abortion Laws</u>" which will kill mostly Black women! Vote to say no to their **<u>KKK</u>** police <u>killing</u> innocent unarmed Nubians and other <u>sick</u>, <u>racist</u> **White supremacy <u>hoax</u>** practices and leave good, decent, regular hard-working people alone; whether their skin-color is Black, Brown, Yellow, Red or White are all **"God's children"** in **His** sight.

Abu Simbel – The "greatest colossal statured" magnificent **temple,** astonishingly carved in a mountain is the "first in the world" has ever seen, is the cover of this "great little book" it seems America's Mount Rushmore imitated, located in **Nubian** peoples "Sub-Saharan Sudan," **Nubia, Africa.** Lower Nubia on the west bank of upper Lake Nasser and across the River Nile from Qasr Ibrim, about 230 km (140 mi) southwest of Aswan and about 190 miles by road, is in Africa just below that borders Egypt.

The **Nubian** monuments are actually two massive carved rock temples out the mountainside in the 13th century BC, during the 19th Dynasty reign of the Pharaoh Ramesses II. The largest is dedicated to the god Amun, as well as to the Pharaoh Ramesses II himself who ordered the creation of the temple. The second, smaller temple is dedicated to the goddess Hathor and Ramesses II's Queen, is his wife Nefertari and children can be seen in smaller figures by his feet.

During the Egyptian Middle Kingdom years of 2040-1640 BC, the Kingdom of Egypt began expanding in **Nubia**. Egyptians gained control over Nubian trade routes and established "fortresses" down the Nile River. There wasn't much interaction (friction) between the two cultures at this time and it was believed to be fairly peaceful. Nubians were known as "fierce warriors" under Egyptian rule, in archery. They were referred to as the **Medjay,** which originally was an area of land where Nubian's lived and then became to mean an "elite" paramilitary force in the Egyptian army.

While Nubians were "Known" for their "Ferocity" in battle, they still worked in all aspects of ancient Egyptian society including as attendants, merchants, temple employees and also menial jobs. Nubians are believed to be one of the oldest ethnic groups along with their oldest neighbor **Ethiopia,** Nubians having a "rich history and culture."

Nubians originate from the 'central Nile valley area,' many Black historian scholars believe to be **Africa's,** "cradle of civilization" and not the many White historian scholars 'Mesopotamia' Middle-East. They played a large role in ancient Egypt and then, during the medieval period, converted to Christianity and formed three kingdoms was **Nobatia, Makuria,** and **Alodia.** Today, the Nubian people practice Islam, and can still be found in the same area from where they originated from in **Sub-Saharan Sudan.** Nubians can be found living in Egypt, Sudan, and even in **Kenya,** which is famous with Nubian historical sites and African Safari as well.

Even though Nubians reside in two different countries, it is important to remember that they retain their own culture, including their own "5" dialect in languages are: **Nobiin, Kenzi, Midob, Birgid,** and **Kordofan** Nubian. Because of their different languages, Egypt employed Nubian speakers as **"code-talkers"** in the Yom Kipper War against **Israel.** Nubians played an important role in the "rise and success" of ancient Egypt and still are an integral part of the country and today's Egyptian tourism.

The **Temple of Beit-Wali-Beital,** is another temple that was built by Ramesses II. Like Abu Simbel, this was one of Ramesses II Nubian temples built in order to try to maintain Egyptian control over Nubia. The first temple to serve this purpose it's believed.

Temple of Dakka – Originally just a small shrine, the temple of Dakka was expanded during the Roman period and was used as a fortress along the Nile River.

Temple of Maharragua – The temple of Maharragua is a small unfinished temple with an unknown history.

Temple of Amada – The temple of Amada is the oldest temple in Nubia. It was built in the 18th dynasty by pharaoh Thutmose III, and dedicated to Amun and Re-Horakhty. Several pharaohs added to this temple over time included Ramesses II.

Temple of Philae – The temple of Philae is in fact, several temples. This site was known as a place where the goddess **Isis** was worshipped. It also was a popular pilgrimage for Nubians, Egyptians, and travelers from as far as **Greece** and **Crete**.

Temple of Kalabsha – The temple of Kalabsha is relatively new in comparison to other Egyptian temples. It was built around 30 BC during the Roman era. The temple was a tribute to the Nubian sun god **Mandulis,** however, it was never completed.

Temple of Derr – The temple of Derr was also constructed by Ramesses II. It's a "rock-cut temple" and was dedicated to Re-Horakhty.

Temple of Wadi as-Subua – Another "rock-cut temple" built by Ramesses II is another of his Nubian temples. Today, it resides in a valley with two New Kingdom temples.

The Qasr Ibrim – Was once a **"fortress"** and a **"major city"** perched on a cliff above the Nile River. Today, after the construction of the dam, Qasr Ibrim is actually situated on a rocky island in the middle of the Nile River. Unfortunately, it can't be visited by tourists.

During his reign, Ramesses II embarked on an extensive building program throughout Nubia and Egypt, to which Egypt controlled. Nubia was very important to the Egyptians because it was a source of **"gold"** and many other precious trade goods. He therefore built, several grand temples in Nubia in order to impress upon the Nubian people Egypt's might and Egyptiantize Nubia.

While the Nubian did introduce some of their culture into Egypt, for the most part they kept the same governing rules, artistic style, temples and religious traditions. During this period of time the Nubians also revived the tradition of **"Pyramid Building."** The Nubians ruled over Egypt (**The 25th Dynasty**) **"for a little over 100 years,"** but were eventually pushed out by the **Assyrians**.

After, being overthrown and pushed out of Egypt the Nubians went back to where they originated from and have essentially stayed in the same area throughout time and can still be found in their home there. Many Egyptian Pharaohs, even prior to the 25th Dynasty, had Nubian **blood** running through their veins. Additionally, **"Egyptian Nubians"** tend to be more socio-economically disadvantaged compared to other cultures in Egypt, and often <u>victims</u> of **'<u>racism</u>.'**

The majority of "Nubian villages" in Egypt today are located near **Aswan** and **Elephantine Island**. These villages are very different than other Egyptian villages and are often easily distinguished from the others by their bright, vibrant colors of green, yellow, red and gold etc. of the houses. Hence, while Nubians who live here are considered to be citizens of Egypt, they still retain their own culture.

An influx of **Arabs** settled in Egypt and the Sudan that means modern day Nubians now follow the **Islamic** faith however, they were convents to Christianity in the "Medieval" period. Nubia, as we know it today, is divided between Sub-Saharan Sudan and Egypt. This happened during the "White man's **colonial** period" and only about a quarter of the Nubian population live in modern Egypt. Again, unfortunately time has not been very kind to Nubians with <u>racism</u> that many were forced to leave their **"homes and villages"** Nubians protest which meant nothing up against "progress" along the Nile River, and so the high **"dam of Aswan"** was built.

Construction of the temple complex started in approximately 1264 BC that lasted for about 20 years. It was known as the "Temple of Ramesses, beloved by Amun." However, with the passage of time, all the temples fell into disuse and eventually became almost covered in **sand.** By the 6th century BC, the **"sand"** had already covered the statues of the main temple up to their knees. The temple complex was forgotten until **1813,** when a **Swiss** researcher Johann Ludwig Burckhardt found the top frieze of the main temple.

In **1959,** an international donations campaign started to save the vitally important historic monuments of Nubia. The southernmost relics of this ancient human civilization wouldn't have been under threat, if not for the construction of the Aswan High Dam with rising water of the Nile.

The salvage of the Abu Simbel temples began in **1964** by a multinational team of archeologists, engineers and skilled heavy equipment operators working together under the UNESCO banner; it cost some $40 million US dollars at the time equal to $300 million in 2017 dollars. Between 1964 and 1968, the entire site was carefully cut into large blocks (up to 30 tons, averaging 20 tons), dismantled, lifted and reassembled in a new location 65 meters (195 feet, a 200 feet high building is 20 stories) higher and 200 meters (600 feet, a football field of 100 yards) from the river, in one of the greatest challenges of archaeological engineering in history. Some structures were even from under the waters of Lake Nasser (they say).

Today, a few hundred tourists visit the temples daily. Many visitors also arrive by plane at an airfield that was specially constructed for the temple complex, or by road from Aswan, the nearest city. The complex consists of two temples. The larger one is dedicated to Ra-Horakhty, Ptah and Amun, Egypt's three state deities of the time, and features four large statues of Ramesses II in the façade same appearance. The smaller temple is dedicated to the goddess Hathor, personified by Nefertari the Queen and Ramesses most beloved of his many wives. The temple at present is open to the public.

Nubian people without a doubt, were very intelligent and an integral part of ancient Egypt as we know it. Savvy, clever, but smart about their valuable goods as tradespeople, incredible merciful warriors, and cunning rulers, the great Nubian people played a large role in the creation and success of ancient Black Egypt. As mentioned before, unfortunately in this article time has not been kind to the Nubian people. And to keep White people **scared** of Black people, is the **bigoted,** White **racist** plan. Who seem today in these **last days,** blatantly dare anyone to do something about it, because they can get away with it, they think always… but **Nubians** are the **phenomenal** "wooly haired people" of **"Alfa and Omega,"** "the beginning and the end" under **God…** His "chosen people" in **His image…**

However, as a tourist you can help so much by taking time to learn more about Nubian culture and pass it on about the "good of a people" and their importance in Egypt, of Nubian Americans, and other Nubians "world-wide." The Nubians of Egypt are a "warm-hearted, kind, and welcoming" people to others, so consider adding a visit to one of their villages into your Egypt tailor made tour.

So ready yourself, to book your trip to Egypt and visit not only the great pyramids but other incredible sites built by Nubians? At **"Osiris Tours,"** we pride ourselves in being one of the best Egypt's luxury tour company, see what you "dreamt" about of histories Nubian **"Abu Simbel."**

Orthodox White man's history is a lie and must be placed back into its proper perspective. A White supremacy veil has thrown us off track somewhat; about world history **"truths"** and who we are as strong Black inventive people they seem to forget, in relationship to everyone else on earth. Whites have many believing they are not only the progenitors (forefather, and originator) of civilization but also the progenitor of **"humanity."** We must first understand in a nutshell Whites are mutated inbred albinos. Since Caucasians cannot reproduce genetic material **"Melanin,"** they could not have spawned (produce or offspring) humanity.

Caucasians birthrates globally are below replacement levels little more than 2%, dwindling also because of their victimization by photolysis. White gene DNA cannot be traced back as far as their genetic parents, BLACK NUBIAN AFRICANS! Because the sun sterilizes and is sending Whites on a course toward extinction, they will not survive independently for very long without people of color depositing their genetic (melanin) material to make their cell replication and reproduction more feasible.

Just about everything we have been led to believe is a myth. White people like to think and want us to believe that they have invented everything that we take for granted in this age. However the truth is, Caucasians have only "REDISCOVERED" the many inventions of OUR BLACK NUBIAN ancestors did **"deep"** in antiquity (prehistory ancient times). Just as they "REDISCOVED AMERICA," with Indian nations already here! Unifying of northern and southern Egypt and Nubia, is preceded by thousands of years of kings that are not taken into account in ancient and prehistory. Egypt did not have a linear (straight) progressive history where they started off primitive and progressed to their ancient history.

NUBIA was the first, then came Egypt as they both started off ADVANCED. Both are the continuation or satellite colonies of an even older and a most fabulous **"super civilization"** everyone, meaning all top nations on earth heard of and are aware of, that Whites erroneously and weren't even created as yet, try pitifully to claim was theirs. There are many ruins and pieces of proof/evidence of the once existence of ATLANTIS.

Not only ancient Plato's account but the megalithic (large or enormous stones used in prehistory monuments) ruins that the United States government is fully aware of off the coast of Bimini. The Bimini Islands, also called Biminis, are a string of Islands, northwestern Bahamas, and West Indies. Bimini is in the Bahamas, only 50 miles away from Miami. Believed to be the remains of the legendary lost empire of Atlantis; that stretches in the Atlantic Ocean easterly in a direction towards our motherland **Africa.**

In perhaps **10,000 BC,** space flight but certainly atomic weapons, may have been the contributing factor in the destruction of Atlantis; is surely a mind-boggling reality with technology similar to we use today in Africa, India, China, Middle East and other South America countries; however, those ruins and pieces of evidence remains have to be the remains of an empire of an ancient **"Black Nubian Civilization,"** that White historians are scared to introduce…perhaps.

There's a 5,000 year old flying machine image etched in a large stone found by American soldiers in an Afghan. Cave. The photographed image source is: Pinterest. Then, Soviet (Russia) scientists discovered old instruments used in navigating cosmic (universe, outer-space) vehicles in caves in **Turkestan** and the **Gobi Desert** (continent of Asia across Mongolia and northwestern China). There are India's Sanskrit texts (there are **five primary sacred texts** of Hinduism), that have references to gods who fought battles in the sky using **Vimana** or (Vimanas) flying vehicles equipped with weapons as deadly as in current times.

Then there's Africa's greatest library at Alexandria that was destroyed by fire that had it not been, for the stupidity from an enemy invasion, the library's contents may have revealed the technology secret of the Black man's use of **"Levitation."** And possible evidence destroyed in <u>hate</u> as well as knowledge in ashes, like India's ancient Indians Viminas flying machine. However, the ancient Indian text from the Ramayana Empire still exists and gives credence to the fact that the Viminas ancient Indian flying machines are a reality and not a figment of some ones imagination.

How old is the Ramayana era? Well, based on astronomical information such as positions of constellations and time of eclipse available in scriptures, they have concluded that events in the Ramayana took place **"7,000 years ago"** and events in the Mahabharata took place **"5,000 years ago.** The Mahabharata <u>war</u> started on October, 3,139 BC. (**5,139 years ago**). White-skin people first appeared on earth **6,000 years ago,** is reasonable could still remember Nubian flying machines handed-down by tribal leader's word of mouth through the generations, and after a while, just didn't let their white masses and others know. It is important that we remember, the inhabitants of the ancient Rama Empire are the ancestors of the Black Dravidians or "Untouchables" (Dalit's) of India today.

It is written in the profound ancient language of Sanskrit, the text give marvelous accounts of really fantastic deadly <u>wars</u> recorded, of strategy fought here on this planet as well as surprisingly in outer space by these ancient flying machines that utilized mercury vortex propulsion. These Vimanas records are not isolated and can be cross-correlated with similar reports in other ancient (like Africa and other) civilizations.

It was also a carefully guarded secret that many of the **"UFO"** sightings of today are actually the **Viminas** of great antiquity being concealed by the United States and other world governments; or reconstructions of those ancient aircrafts is todays, USAF once top secret **"nuclear"** powered **"Flying Triangle"** – **TR-3B**. The alleged mercury vortex engine that generates a magnetic vortex which effectively neutralizes the effects of gravity on mass.

And so you don't think this is fantasy fiction, we're putting aside human DNA at this time and we'll DNA this flying machine so to speak. A real machinery genetics of mechanical technology we'll call it. Without further delay, the TR-3B is code name for the **Astra,** which is no make believe. The triangular shaped nuclear powered aero-spacecraft platform was developed Top Secret. At least 3 of the **billion** dollar plus TR-3Bs were flying by "1994." The Aurora is the most classified aerospace development program in in existence. The craft is funded and operationally tasked by the National Reconnaissance Office, the NSA, and the **CIA.**

A circular, plasma filled accelerator ring called the Magnetic Field Disrupter, is far ahead of any imaginable technology. The plasms, **mercury** based, is pressurized at **250,000 atmosphere** at a temperature of 150 degrees Kelvin (a temperature scale, which absolute zero is O-K the equivalent of **-273.15 degrees C**) and accelerated to **50,000 rpm** to create a super-conductive plasma with the resulting **"gravity disruption."**

The MFD generates a magnetic vortex field, which disrupts or neutralizes the effects of gravity on mass within proximity, by **89%**. Do not, misunderstand this is **"not anti-gravity"** that provides a repulsive force, that can be used for propulsion. The mass of the circular accelerator and all mass weight within the accelerator, such as the crew capsule, avionics (electronics designed for use in aerospace vehicles), MFD systems, fuels crew environmental systems, and the heavy nuclear reactor, weights are all reduced by **89%,** and the craft can travel at **Mach 9** (7,000 to 8,000 mph), vertically or horizontally. Sources say the performance is not limited to stresses that the human pilots can endure considering the **89%** reduction in mass; the **"G forces"** are also reduced by **89%!!!**

The TR-3Bs propulsion is provided by **3 multimode thrusters** mounted under each corner, of the triangular platform. The TR-3B is a **sub-Mach 9** vehicle until it reaches altitudes above **120,000 feet,** then God knows how fast it can go! The **3 multimode rocket engines** mounted under each corner of the craft uses hydrogen or methane and oxygen as a propellant.

In a liquid oxygen/hydrogen rocket system, 85% of the propellant mass is oxygen. The nuclear thermal rocket engine uses a hydrogen propellant, augmented with oxygen for additional thrust. The reactor heats the liquid hydrogen and injects liquid oxygen in the supersonic nozzle, so that the hydrogen burns concurrently in the liquid oxygen afterburner. The multimode propulsion system can ; operate in the atmosphere, with thrust provided by the nuclear reactor, in the upper atmosphere, with hydrogen propulsion, and in orbit, with the combined hydrogen/oxygen propulsion. Remember, the **3 rocket engines** are reportedly built by Rockwell. Many sightings of triangular **UFOs** are not "alien" vehicles but the top secret, **TR-3B.**

Creating the TR-3B, modified to the **"TR-3A,"** added on to confuse further the fact that each of these designators is a different aircraft and not the same aerospace vehicle. A TR-3B is as different from a TR-3A as a banana is from a grape. Some of these vehicles are manned and others are unmanned. And in closing here, we at the *Fortney Encyclical History Ed. Co.* realize this has been for you an unexpected reality learning, and an enjoyed great enlightenment in reading. So stay strong, stay wise, have eyes in the back of your head and **fair-you-well!**

Did You Know This? Africa's great civilizations made an immense contribution to the world, which are still marveled at by people today but those who marvel and many more perhaps do NOT know that **"Africans Are the World's First Seafarers."** Africans crossed the Atlantic Ocean and reached the American continent, perhaps even North America as early as **500 BC**. In the **14th century**, the **Syrian** writer al-Umari, wrote about the voyage of the Emperor of Mali who crossed the Atlantic with **2,000 ships** but failed to return.

Africans in east and southeastern Africa also set up great

civilizations that established important trading links with the kingdoms and empires of **India** and **China** long before Caucasian Europeans had learned from the Africans how to navigate the Atlantic Ocean. When Europeans first sailed to Africa in the **15th century**, African pilots and **navigators** "<u>shared</u>" with them their knowledge of trans-oceanic travel.

It was **"gold"** from the great empires of West Africa, Ghana, Mali and Songhay, which provided the means for the economic take-off of Europe in the **13th** and **14th centuries** and aroused the interest of Europeans in Western Africa. An early historian in the **9th century** wrote *"The king of Ghana is a great king. In his territory are mines of gold."* When the famous historian of Muslim Spain, al-Bakri wrote about Ghana in the **11th** century, he reports that its king *"rules an enormous kingdom and has great power."* The king was said to have an army of **200,000** men to rule over an extremely wealthy empire (by the way, President Obama withdrew **150,000** American troops from **Iraq**).

In the **14th century**, the West African empire of **Mali** was larger than Western Europe and reputed to be one of the "largest," "richest" and "most powerful" states in the "**world!**" When the famous emperor of Mali, "**Mansa Musa**" visited **Cairo**, Egypt in **1324**, it was said that he brought so much gold with him that its price fell so dramatically it did not recover its value until **12 years later**.

The empire of **Songhay** was known, amongst other noted things, for the famous world's first university of Sankore based in and called Timbuctu (Timbuktu or Timbuktoo)." Aristotle was studied at **Sankore**, "**Timbuktu**" with subjects like law, various branches of philosophy, dialectic, grammar, rhetoric and astronomy. In the **16th century**, one of its most famous scholars, Ahmed Baba, is said to have written more than **40** major books on subjects such as astronomy, history and theology and he had his own private library that held over **1,500 volumes**.

The Muslim invasion of Europe, and the founding of the state of Cordoba, re-introduced all the learning of the ancient world as well as the various contributions made by Islamic scholars and linked Europe much more closely with North and West Africa. So important was the knowledge found in **Muslim Spain**, that one Christian Monk – Adelard of Bath – disguised himself as a Muslim in order to study at the university at Cordoba. Many historians believe that it was this knowledge of **"Muslims"** and definitely the **"African Moors"** brought to Europe through Spain, which not only created the conditions for the **Renaissance** during the middle-ages but also for the eventual expansion of Europe's beginning after Africa's seafaring voyages overseas to the Americas in the last **14th** and early **15th century**.

****

Did You Know This? A stout, stand-fast **"Healing Process Remedy for Racism"****** starts with **"Mending Not Avenging History"** either's-way. A **"Mending Anti-African Holocaust In History Academics"** – is with an **"African American Filming Industry;"** interest in achievement movies by **"African American Historians,"** beginnings shown in grammar, high school, and higher schools of education. This would have almost endless topics of the arts and sciences that eventually could spill over into outside entertainment films of authentic histories "War and Peace".

An African American owned filming industry, would be accomplished almost over-night by all players who are champions of big money-making in **"sports."** Our football, baseball, basketball etc. and with the **"Arts"** champions of music's Hip-Hop, Rock & Roll, musician and **"Acting"** stars all together becoming champion contributors; would become **"heroic"** examples, buying mass **share certificates** in their corporate investment of naming perhaps

"HISTORY INC." an **African American Movie Industry**.

A beginning of academic historical African awareness, short episodes "identity movies" for grammar, then high school and pre-higher schools in public education.

"Biblical Israel Was the Land of Cush"

During the millennial reign of Nubian wooly-hair Christ, an activist liberator for his people, the people, the poor and children Jesus called in anger, "suffer little children to come unto me, and forbid them not: for such is the kingdom of God." Jesus Christ loved and honored little children. Jesus will receive honor from Cush/Ethiopia: "From beyond the rivers of Cush my worshipers, my scattered people, will bring me offerings" (Zephaniah 3:10).

The **Bible** is a reliable, **eyewitness** history criteria of **origin.** Don't over-play leaving no stone unturned towards an advanced lifestyle driven by need. Nubian Americans DNA have much to rise from and **lead** into the **1,000-year period of peace and righteousness** following the second return; of wooly-hair **Nubian Jesus Christ,** who will **"reign"** over the earth during that time...

THE END... "Begins the **American Nubians** being phenomenal people"

ILLUSTRATIONS

He ain't heavy He's my brother
Africa under full glacial conditions
Egypt Sinai Peninsula
     ****

Egyptians and the Great White Race Map
The ancient connection of Northeast Africa
The Crucifixion
Moses the Law Giver
     ****

Our Precious Children
3,000 Years Old Helicopter, Submarine ETC.
The Sacred Black Madonna
Akebu-Lan means "Mother of Mankind" Map
Ancient Map of Continental Africa
     ****

Nubia Region Today Map
Nubian Meroe Pyramids
Ramesses II Storming the Hittite Fortress of Dapur
The Great Nubian is Before the Egyptians
The Giza plateau 3 predominant Pyramids & Great Sphinx
25th Nubian Dynasty/Kushite Tadja
Nubian Winged Goddess
     ****

REFERENCES
(Nubian American Identity Rise DNA Proof)

The Fortney Encyclical History Ed. Co. – The World's True Black History, *"First Edition"* by Albert Fortney Jr. 2015; The African Chronologic History is Bible, *"Second Edition"* by Albert Fortney Jr. 2017; The New School Untold History *"Third Edition"* by Albert Fortney Jr. 2019; A Child's Short History Book ***Black History Month African Study"*** (In cartoon animal characters) by Albert Fortney Jr. 2014; Gold & High-Tech of The Gods *"Fortney Encyclical High-Tech Science"* by Albert Fortney Jr. 2020.

R.T. P Prittchett, scientist in his book, "Natural History of Man," Egyptians was an African Race"

Anthropologist – Count Constain de Volney (1727-1820

Yakub (Nation of Islam) – Wikipedia, the free encyclopedia, Hon. Elijah Muhammad – (expert statements), Hon. Louis Farrakhan – (excerpt statements)

Anthony T. Brower – "Exploding the Myths Vol. 1 Nile Valley Contributions to Civilization"

The Psychology of Racism defining Black History – "Special thanks goes out to," Denzel Caldwell, Nawal Mustafa, Edwin Smit (excerpts total a page)

"Blacked-Out Through Whitewash" by SuZar (r. Epp) Su Zar.com, with thanks from "The New School Untold History" by Albert Fortney Jr. (the grand historian author)

Lepore, J. (2020, July 13). The Invention of the Police. Newyorker. https://www.newyorker.com/magazine/2020/07/20/the-invention-of-the-police

Wikipedia contributors. (2022, September 25). Abu Simbel. In *Wikipedia, The Free Encyclopedia*. Retrieved 20:55, October 3, 2022, from https://en.wikipedia.org/w/index.php?title=Abu_Simbel&oldid=1112245325

Thanks goes out to: Spread the Love – African Tribes descendants of the Hebrew Nation by Nana Kofi

REFERENCES
(Let Us Make Man)

Anthony T. Brower – "Exploding the Myths Vol. 1 Nile Valley Contributions to Civilization"

Anthropologist – Count Constain de Volney (1727-1820)

"Blacked-Out Through Whitewash" by SuZar (r. Epp) Su Zar.com with
Thanks from "The New School Untold history, *"Third Edition"* by Albert Fortney Jr. 2019 (the grand historian author)

Murfin, B. (1992, March 26-29). African Science in School Curriculum, University of Pennsylvania – African Studies Center. African Science in
School Curriculum (upenn.edu)

R. T. Prittchett, scientist in his book, "Natural History of Man," Egyptians were an African Race"

The Psychology of Racism defining Black History – "Special thanks Goes out to, Denzel Caldwell, Nawal Mustafa, Edwin Smit"

Yakub (Nation of Islam) – Wikipedia, the free encyclopedia, Hon. Elijah Muhammad – (expert statement), Minister Malcolm X "Let Us Make Man"

Thanks goes out to Roxana Sinex, great art picture of books Back cover exceptional "Nubian Warrior Queen Amanirenas"

Your host and historian author: Albert Fortney Jr. (O. G. Al), I.Q. 125+ institution recorded, capacity C.E.O. in insurance… At 19 yrs. old passed Denver, Colorado civil service exam. Test with 98% correct. Qualified OSHA inspector – Has-mat Training local 472 Newark, NJ. This journey in life molded me and contributed to writing this vitally important book in these troubling day's and time will end of lies; back to the beginning with truth today and the future return to black people. God bless America's "we the people" real history.

www.ingramcontent.com/pod-product-compliance
Lightning Source LLC
Chambersburg PA
CBHW051906160426
43198CB00012B/1767